The
TAX
Treatment
of
Fringe
Benefits

Stephen A. Woodbury
and
Wei-Jang Huang

1991

W. E. UPJOHN INSTITUTE for Employment Research
Kalamazoo, Michigan

Library of Congress Cataloging-in-Publication Data

Woodbury, Stephen A.
    The tax treatment of fringe benefits / Stephen A. Woodbury and Wei-Jang
Huang.
        p.   cm.
    Includes bibliographical references and index.
    ISBN 0-88099-107-0 (acid-free). — ISBN 0-88099-108-9 (pbk. : acid-free)
    1. Employee fringe benefits—Taxation—United States—Econometric
models.   I. Huang, Wei-Jang.   II. Title.
    HJ4653.F7W66 1991
    336.24'22—dc20   91-6792
                                                                                  CIP

Cover design by J.R. Underhill
Index prepared by Shirley Kessel
Printed in the United States of America

THE AUTHORS

Stephen A. Woodbury is an Associate Professor of Economics at Michigan State University and a Senior Economist at the W. E. Upjohn Institute. He received his A.B. degree from Middlebury College in 1975 and his Ph.D. in Economics from the University of Wisconsin in 1981. His recent publications include "Controlled Experiments and the Unemployment Insurance System," in *Unemployment Insurance: The Second Half-Century* (1990), and "Economic Issues in Employee Benefits," in *Research in Labor Economics* (1990)..

Wei-Jang Huang is a research analyst with the W. E. Upjohn Institute. She received her B.A. degree from National Taiwan University in 1977 and her M.A. in Economics from the University of California at Santa Barbara in 1980. She has co-authored two other articles with Stephen Woodbury on fringe benefits, including "An Evaluation of Proposals to Tax Employer Contributions to Voluntary Pension and Health Insurance Plans" in *New Issues in Wages, Non-Wages and Employment* (1989).

ACKNOWLEDGMENTS

It is a pleasure to thank those who have helped us in various ways with the work presented here. The project would not have been undertaken without the financial support of the Office of the Assistant Secretary for Planning and Evaluation (ASPE), U.S. Department of Health and Human Services. We are grateful for that support, and to the grant monitors at ASPE—Robert Schmitt, Paul Hughes-Cromwick, and Michele Adler—who advised, encouraged, and prodded us during a rather long gestation period. The support of the W. E. Upjohn Institute was essential to completion of the monograph. We are grateful to Wayne Wendling, who participated in the planning of the project and would have continued with it had he remained at the Upjohn Institute. We thank Michigan Third District Congressman Howard Wolpe and his staff for helping us gain access to the Health Insurance/Employer Survey component of the National Medical Care Expenditure Survey, which we use in chapter 3.

Many friends and associates have helped us by discussing our work in progress and offering advice: Carl Davidson, John H. Goddeeris, Daniel S. Hamermesh, Andrew J. Hogan, and Paul L. Menchik (all of Michigan State University); H. Allan Hunt, Timothy L. Hunt, and Robert G. Spiegelman (all of the W. E. Upjohn Institute); David N. F. Bell, Robert A. Hart, and Seiichi Kawasaki (all of the University of Stirling, Scotland); Emily S. Andrews (University of Rhode Island), B. K. Atrostic (U.S. Department of the Treasury), Olivia Mitchell (Cornell University), Alicia H. Munnell (Federal Reserve Bank of Boston), Donald O. Parsons (The Ohio State University), Susan Pozo (Western Michigan University), Joseph F. Quinn (Boston College), Frank A. Scott (University of Kentucky), Daniel J. Slottje (Southern Methodist University), John A. Turner (U.S. Department of Labor), and Robert W. Turner (Colgate University). Our thanks to all.

We are especially grateful to William T. Alpert (University of Connecticut and William H. Donner Foundation) for his helpful advice at nearly every stage of the project, and for his extraordinarily careful reading of an early draft of the manuscript which resulted in many substantive changes and a complete rewriting. We also received helpful criticism from seminar participants at Michigan State University and the W. E. Upjohn Institute, and from conference participants at the European Communities' Conference on New Issues in Wages, Nonwages, and Employment and various annual meetings of the Midwest Economics Association and Eastern Economic Association.

Ellen Maloney handled innumerable details of producing the manuscript, Judy Gentry edited it, and Shirley Kessel produced the index. Many thanks to each. We also thank Azman bin Abdullah, Eric Chua, and James Stansell, who helped us with data at various stages.

During the time we worked on this monograph, we are fortunate indeed to have had the support of our families: Susan Pozo, Ricardo Pozo Woodbury, and Wei-Chiao, Charissa, and Jasmine Huang.

POLICY SUMMARY

A multitude of public policy issues currently surround the tax treatment of employee benefits. In particular, the tax-favored status of employer contributions to pensions and health insurance has been blamed for numerous ills: a shrinking tax base that has exacerbated the federal budget deficit; an inefficient and bloated health care sector; overinsurance by many recipients of employer-provided health insurance; rising health care costs; and a tax system that is made more regressive because those who receive tax-favored fringe benefits tend to be in higher-income households than those who do not.

This study investigates how possible changes in the tax treatment of fringe benefits—mainly pensions and health insurance—can be expected to influence the provision of benefits by employers. We develop a model of fringe benefit provision in the United States, estimate that model using two separate data sets, and use the estimates to simulate how various proposed changes in federal personal income tax policy would affect the provision of private pensions and health insurance, the mix of employee compensation, federal revenues, and income inequality.

Estimates of the model of fringe benefits suggest three points about workers' preferences for wages and fringe benefits. First, the demand for pensions and health insurance is highly responsive to changes in total compensation (is income elastic), whereas the demand for wage and salary payments is rather unresponsive to changes in total compensation (is income inelastic). Hence, if compensation were to double, pensions and health insurance would more than double, but wages would less than double. Second, workers view both pensions and health insurance as good substitutes for wages, and probably view pensions as a better substitute for wages than health insurance. Third, workers may view pensions and health insurance as complements, so that more of one results in a greater demand for the other.

We use one of our estimated models to simulate the effects of three major changes in tax policy: (a) the Tax Reform Act of 1986, which significantly lowered the marginal tax rates facing most households; (b) treating employer contributions to health insurance as taxable income, but leaving employer contributions to pensions untaxed (we consider separately the consequences of taxing all health insurance contributions and of taxing only contributions in excess of $1,125 annually); and (c) treating employer contributions to both pensions and health insurance as taxable income.

The simulations suggest that the Tax Reform Act of 1986 has increased real expenditures on health insurance provided by employers and shifted the mix of compensation away from pensions and toward health insurance. This may seem paradoxical, because the 1986 tax reform reduced the incentive to demand fringe benefits (including health insurance) by lowering marginal tax rates on wage income. The increase in health insurance provision is attributable to the large (positive) income effects of the tax reform. The simulations also suggest that the 1986 tax reform has reduced personal income tax revenues by over 21 percent, and has had minimal distributional effects.

We find that treating all health insurance contributions as taxable income would reduce real expenditures on employer-provided health insurance by nearly 15 percent, and that taxing health insurance contributions in excess of $1,125 per year (in 1982 dollars) would reduce health insurance by nearly 9 percent. Taxing health insurance would also result in relatively small reductions in employer-provided pensions. Income tax revenues would increase by 8 percent annually if all health insurance contributions were taxed, and by 1.5 percent if contributions over $1,125 were taxed. Taxing all health insurance contributions would have little effect on income equality, but a low tax cap would increase income equality.

Finally, we find that taxing all fringe benefits would cut pension provision in half and health insurance provision by 20 percent. Taxing all fringe benefits would increase income tax revenues by over 17 percent and would increase income equality.

We believe that taxing both pensions and health insurance is too sweeping a policy change to implement in the foreseeable future: our estimates suggest that taxing all fringe benefits would cut employer contributions to pensions nearly in half. Also, although mandated health insurance is not a topic of our empirical work, we believe that too little research has been conducted on mandated health insurance to inform good decisionmaking, and that requiring employers to provide health insurance could create its own set of problems without providing a complete solution to the problems it is intended to address.

In contrast, we believe that taxing health insurance contributions in excess of some relatively low amount (a tax cap on health insurance contributions of $1,125 in 1982 dollars, or about $1,500 in current dollars) would be an economically sensible and efficiency-improving policy. A low tax cap on health insurance would partially address the problems of rising health care costs and overuse of the health care system, would prevent further erosion of the income tax base, would not limit or reduce access to basic health insurance benefits by currently insured or potentially insurable workers, and would increase income equality.

viii

CONTENTS

TABLES

1

Introduction

Issues in the Tax Treatment of Fringe Benefits

In the United States, a significant proportion of retirement income and health insurance benefits are provided through private pension and health insurance plans to which employers contribute voluntarily. In 1987, 31 percent of all retirement benefits came from private pension plans, and roughly two-thirds of all expenditures on health and medical care were private.[1] This private approach to providing retirement income and health care differs markedly from many other western nations, where far greater proportions of retirement income and health care are provided by public programs.

The private provision of pension and health benefits in the U.S. has been stimulated and encouraged by the tax system.[2] Whereas wage income is taxed under the federal personal income tax, employer contributions to pensions and health insurance plans are excluded from taxable income.[3] An accumulating body of empirical research has suggested that this favorable tax treatment of fringe benefits has created an effective incentive to substitute fringe benefits for wages, and that much of the growth of private pension and health insurance plans can be attributed to that favorable tax treatment (see below for a discussion of this research).

The favorable tax treatment of employer contributions to voluntary fringe benefit plans in the United States has been under attack since at least 1973, when Martin Feldstein argued that the exclusion of health insurance contributions from taxable income distorts the incentive to demand health insurance and leads to overuse of the health care system. One aspect of Feldstein's argument was that the tax-favored status of health insurance is responsible for the rising cost of medical care. That is, since the tax system creates an incentive to buy more health insurance, and since health insurance coverage leads to greater use of the health care system, the tax-favored status of health insurance drives up both the demand for health care and the cost of health care (Feldstein 1973; Vogel 1980). Another aspect of Feldstein's argument was that tax subsidies for health insurance are inefficient: the government could provide the same amount of health care directly, finance the health care through lump-sum taxes, and have revenue left over that could be returned to taxpayers or used to buy other public goods or services.

Somewhat different arguments have been made against continuing the tax-favored status of private pensions in the United States. Alicia Munnell has been a vocal proponent of taxing pension contributions, arguing that the tax-favored treatment of pensions has resulted in erosion of the income and payroll tax bases and a more regressive tax system (Munnell 1984, 1985). As the growth of pension contributions has slowed (Woodbury and Huang 1988), this argument has lost some of its force. But more recently, Munnell (1988, 1989) has generally criticized the private pension system in the U.S. on the grounds that it covers too small a proportion of households, reduces mobility of the workforce, and provides benefits whose real purchasing power is vulnerable to inflation. Her arguments suggest that a smaller private pension system would be desirable, and taxing employer contributions to private pensions is clearly one possible way of reducing the importance of the private pension system in the United States.

Existing Research and the Need for Further Work

Although fringe benefits have been the subject of a growing body of literature, a limited number of studies have examined the influence of favorable tax treatment of benefits on benefit levels or on the mix of total compensation—those that do being Alpert (1983), Atrostic (1983), Hamermesh and Woodbury (1990), Holmer (1984), Leibowitz (1983), Long and Scott (1982), Rice (1966a, 1966b), Sloan and Adamache (1986), Taylor and Wilensky (1983), Turner (1987), Vroman and Anderson (1984), Woodbury (1983), and Woodbury and Huang (1988). Some additional studies (Goldstein and Pauly 1976; Mumy and Manson 1985) have attempted to draw inferences about the effects of taxes on benefits, but have done so without including explicit tax measures.

The studies that include explicit tax measures take essentially one of two empirical approaches. The first approach is to regress (for an individual or a group) a measure of the *level* of employer contributions to all fringe benefits (*FB*), or pension benefits (*PB*), or health insurance benefits (*HB*) on a measure of the marginal tax rate facing the group (or individual) and a vector of control variables:

$$FB = a_0 + a_1 t + a_2 x_2 + \ldots + a_m x_m + e_f \qquad (1.1)$$

$$PB = b_0 + b_1 t + b_2 x_2 + \ldots + b_m x_m + e_p \qquad (1.2)$$

$$HB = c_0 + c_1 t + c_2 x_2 + \ldots + c_m x_m + e_h, \qquad (1.3)$$

where t is the marginal tax rate facing the group or individual, the x_i represent $(m-1)$ control variables, the a_i, b_i, and c_i are coefficients, and the e_i are normally distributed error terms. This procedure or some variant of it is followed by Atrostic (1983), Leibowitz (1983), Rice (1966a, 1966b), Sloan and Adamache (1986), Taylor and Wilensky (1983), and Vroman and Anderson (1984).

The alternative approach is to use as a dependent variable in equations like (1.1), (1.2), and (1.3) not the *level* of benefits per worker, but the *share* of total compensation received by workers as fringe benefits, pension benefits, or contributions to health insurance. Usually these shares are constructed in the following way:

$$FB/TC = FB/(FB + WS) \qquad (1.4)$$

$$PB/TC = PB/(PB + WS) \qquad (1.5)$$

$$HB/TC = HB/(HB + WS), \qquad (1.6)$$

where *TC* refers to total compensation per worker, and *WS* is wage and salary payments per worker. This approach or some variant of it is taken by Alpert (1983), Hamermesh and Woodbury (1990), Long and Scott (1982), Sloan and Adamache (1986), Turner (1987), Woodbury (1983), and Woodbury and Huang (1988). One possible advantage of this latter approach is that it can be shown to have an explicit link to well-known consumer theoretic models (Woodbury 1983).

These two approaches and the studies based on them share an important weakness, correction of which could improve both our basic understanding of benefit provision and our predictions about how policy changes would affect benefit provision. Essentially, no study has considered that different benefits have different costs, and that cost differences between benefits may vary over time, by size of firm, and by region. As a result, no study to date has been able to estimate a tradeoff between any *pair* of fringe benefits (for example, between pensions and health insurance). The implication is that no study to date has estimated the effect of a change in tax policy that is specific to just one benefit (a tax cap on health insurance contributions, for example) on the amount of some other benefit provided by the employer.[4] Neither has existing work shown whether the impact of taxing both pensions and health insurance would have a different impact on the provision of pensions than on the provision of health insurance.

The same weakness implies that existing studies may have obtained biased estimates of tax effects on fringe benefits as a whole (or on a single specific benefit). In effect, as will be shown in chapter 2, the existing studies have made questionable simplifying assumptions about the rate at which the employer is willing to trade pensions for health insurance. This leads to an omitted variables bias that could, in principle, lead to mistaken inferences about the relation between taxes and fringe benefits.

Another weakness shared by most previous studies is that they have had difficulty separating income effects from tax (or price-substitution) effects on the provision of nonwage benefits. In some studies, income effects are ignored, and in most studies where they are distinguished, collinearity between income and marginal tax rates has frustrated the effort to distinguish income from substitution effects. In this monograph, we use both a pooled time-series of cross sections, and a cross section of establishments, in an attempt to obtain improved and robust estimates of income and substitution effects.

In summary, the need for further work is clear. Both because of the scarcity of studies on the effect of taxes on the mix of total compensation, and because of certain weaknesses in the studies that do exist, this area of research remains in an early stage. No study to date has examined how taxing pension contributions would affect the private provision of pensions. Also, even though some studies have examined how taxing health insurance contributions might influence private health insurance (Taylor and Wilensky 1983; Phelps 1984–85; Adamache and Sloan 1985), the existing studies have not taken account of the presence of pensions in the compensation package. Doing so could be important for at least two reasons. First, the relationship of substitutability or complementarity between pensions and health insurance could imply that taxing health contributions would have a significant impact on the provision of pensions by employers. Second, if a tax cap on health insurance did affect pension provision, then it would be important to take account of that effect in determining the revenue effects of taxing health contributions. Failure to do so could lead to either an under- or overestimate of the revenues to be raised by taxing health insurance contributions.

Plan of the Monograph

It is not our intent to offer a comprehensive treatment of the economics of fringe benefits in this monograph.[5] Rather, we have two goals that are more specific and more modest. The first is to obtain estimates of tradeoffs among wages, pensions, and health insurance that are an improvement over existing estimates. In particular, we have tried to produce convincing estimates of the degree to which pensions (individually) and health insurance (individually) are substitutes for wages, and of whether pensions and health insurance are substitutes, complements, or unrelated. Such estimates have not been obtained before in a general framework that considers wages, pensions, and health insurance all at once.

Chapter 2 offers a detailed treatment of the model of fringe benefit provision that we use to estimate tradeoffs among wages, pensions, and health insurance. The result of that chapter is an econometric specification that allows us to estimate substitution (or tax) effects and income effects on the provision of fringe benefits. In chapter 3, we describe the data used to estimate the model and report the results of estimation. We use two separate data sets to estimate our model. The first is a pooled time-series of cross sections (1969–1982) from the National Income and Product Accounts "other labor income" series. The second is a cross section of establishments from the 1977 Survey of Employer Expenditures for Employee Compensation.

Our second main goal is to use the estimates we produce to simulate the effects of various policy changes on the provision of fringe benefits. In chapter 4, we simulate how three major changes in tax policy would affect the voluntary provision by employers of pensions and health benefits. The changes simulated are: (a) the 1986 tax reform, which substantially lowered the marginal tax rates on earnings faced by many households; (b) treating employer contributions to health insurance as taxable income (we simulate both a policy of taxing all contributions to health insurance and a policy of taxing only contributions in excess of $1,125 per year); and (c) treating all employer contributions to both pensions and health insurance as taxable income.

Chapter 5 offers a summary of the model, our empirical findings, and our simulations. We also develop the implications of our findings for public policy in chapter 5.

NOTES

[1] These figures were computed from data in tables 3.A3 and 3.A4 of the *Social Security Bulletin Annual Statistical Supplement*, 1989. Roughly half of all private expenditures on health care were made through employer-provided health insurance. See Kasper, Rossiter, and Wilson (1987); and U.S. Department of Commerce, Bureau of Economic Analysis (1986) and *Survey of Current Business* (various July issues), table 6.13.

[2] Congressional Budget Office (1987) and Atrostic and Burman (1988) raise and provide excellent discussions of the policy issues surrounding the tax treatment of pensions and other fringe benefits. Mitchell (1988) offers a concise introduction.

[3] On the development of the tax code as it bears on pensions and health insurance in the United States, see Korczak (1984, Chap. 2) and Chollet (1984, Chap. 4). See Organization for Economic

Cooperation and Development (1988) for a discussion of the tax treatment of fringe benefits in OECD member countries.

Although neither pension nor health-insurance contributions are taxable to workers at the time they are made, pension benefits are taxable when they are received in retirement. Accordingly, pensions are often referred to as tax-deferred benefits, whereas health insurance, which is never taxed, is referred to as a tax-exempt benefit. See Korczak (1984, pp. 3–10) for a discussion.

[4] Taylor and Wilensky (1983), Phelps (1984–85), and Adamache and Sloan (1985) offer estimates of the revenue effects of taxing health benefits; however, because they consider only tradeoffs between health benefits and wages, these studies are open to the criticism that they overstate the revenue gains of taxing health contributions.

[5] See Hart (1984) and Hart, Bell, Frees, Kawasaki, and Woodbury (1988) for broader views of the economics of ncnwages.

2

A Model of Fringe Benefit Provision

The mix of fringe benefits and wages in the compensation package depends jointly on the decisions of employers and employees, both of whom operate under two sets of constraints. The first set of constraints can be thought of as market constraints associated with factor prices, goods prices, technology, and incomes. The second can be thought of as constraints (or incentives) established by government, with tax policies and the Employee Retirement Income Security Act (ERISA) being the two outstanding examples. Thus, although the employer actually provides the compensation package, that package must be fashioned subject to the preferences of workers (who can alter their level of effort or seek employment elsewhere if a compensation package is unsuitable) and subject to government policies (for example, meeting ERISA vesting, funding, fiduciary, and reporting standards if a defined-benefit pension plan is part of the compensation package). All these factors then — workers' preferences, employers' costs, and government policy — must be a part of any overarching theory of fringe benefit determination.

It is convenient to model the determination of fringe benefits by supposing that the employer offers a menu of possible benefit packages — or at least is willing to offer a variety of benefit packages — and that workers select the package they most prefer. Institutionally, this may seem somewhat unrealistic, because we normally picture the employer making the benefit determination unilaterally — the worker must take or leave whatever is offered.[1] But employers do fashion their benefit packages with the preferences of workers in mind; indeed, if they failed to do so, they would find themselves with a level of labor turnover higher than desired, or a workforce of lesser quality than desired. An important advantage of casting the problem in this way is that it allows us to make use of the large theoretical and applied literature on consumer theory, which is one of the main developments of modern economics (see, for example, the excellent texts by Deaton and Muellbauer 1980b; Phlips 1983; and Theil 1980). So, although modeling fringe benefits as "chosen" by workers may seem somewhat inconsistent with the institutional realities of the process of benefit provision, it does little violence to our ability to predict benefit outcomes as long as we take full account of the constraints and costs faced by the employer in deciding what benefit packages are acceptable.

All existing research that attempts to model explicitly the mix of compensation approaches the problem as one where employees maximize utility by selecting from among a variety of possibilities presented by the employer (see Alpert 1983; Freeman 1981; Sloan and Adamache 1986; Smeeding 1983; Triplett 1983; and Woodbury 1983, for example). The reason is that much of this existing work has focused on the responses of workers to the favorable tax treatment that nonwage benefits receive under the federal personal income tax. There is no convenient way of modeling this aspect of benefit determination through an approach that focuses on the employer.[2] However, nothing in the utility-maximization approach commonly used precludes complete consideration of the factors determining the employer's willingness to offer benefits.

In the remainder of this chapter, a model developed previously to describe the tradeoff between wages and fringes (Woodbury 1983) is extended to include tradeoffs between a *pair* of fringe benefits. The model developed is a utility-maximizing model that restricts attention to the determination of wages and the two most important voluntarily provided fringe benefits: pension plans and insurance contributions (most of which are for health care). Employer contributions to social security, unemployment insurance, and workers' compensation are not determined within the model because provision of these benefits is legally mandated and beyond the scope of the firm's decision.[3] Neither is the consumption by workers of goods such as food and clothing determined within the model because no available data set includes data on both goods consumption and fringe benefit consumption.

Heuristic Statement of the Model

Consider that there are only three forms of compensation: wage benefits, pension benefits, and health insurance benefits. Consider also that the worker's utility depends on the *quantities* of goods bought with wage benefits (z_w), pensions or retirement benefits (z_r), and health insurance benefits (z_h):

$$U = U(z_w, z_r, z_h). \qquad (2.1)$$

A worker chooses quantities of z_w, z_r, and z_h so as to maximize utility subject to a budget constraint that can be written:

$$z_w p_w + z_r p_r + z_h p_h = m. \qquad (2.2)$$

In equation (2.2), p_w, p_r, and p_h are the prices of wage goods, pension or retirement benefits, and health insurance benefits, each of which is beyond the worker's control. Also, m is the maximum dollar amount that the employer is willing to expend on workers' wages, pensions, and health insurance. Although m excludes various components of compensation such as social security and in-kind perquisites, it will be referred to as *total compensation* in what follows.[4]

Stated in this way, the problem of fringe benefit choice is a straightforward problem of consumer demand and may be handled by well-known techniques. But two basic difficulties need to be overcome. First, we do not ordinarily observe *quantities* of the components of compensation (z_w, z_r, and z_h) or the prices of those components (p_w, p_r, and p_h). We do observe the dollar amounts expended by employers on the various components of compensation. For example, $p_w z_w$ would be the number of dollars paid to a worker in wages, and $p_r z_r$ would be the dollar contribution to the worker's pension plan. But prices and quantities must be observed separately in order to estimate some representation of the utility function (eq. 2.1). Accordingly, if the consumer model is to be made workable in this application, some effort will need to be spent identifying and measuring either the quantities or the prices of the components of compensation. Measurement of these prices is discussed further in a later section of this chapter and in the appendix to chapter 3.

The second difficulty to overcome is that the budget constraint (eq. 2.2) turns out to have some unconventional features that require careful treatment. In discussing these unconventional features, it is useful to proceed in two steps. First, we examine the tradeoff between wages and either of the two fringe benefit goods—pensions or health insurance. This allows us to focus on the fact that wages are taxed, whereas fringe benefits are not, and to draw out the implications of this difference in tax treatment. Second, we examine the tradeoff between pensions and health insurance. This allows us to focus on the differences in the employer's cost of providing different fringe benefits, and to draw out the implications of these cost differences for fringe benefit demand.

Wage Taxation and the Tradeoff
Between Wages and Fringe Benefits

Suppose for the moment that the quantity of health insurance benefits has already been determined and is held fixed. This allows us to analyze substitution between wage benefits and pension benefits in a two-dimensional diagram such as figure 2.1, which depicts a representative worker's preferences for pension and wage benefits.[5] The quantity of wage benefits (z_w) is measured along the horizontal axis, and the quantity of pension benefits (z_r) along the vertical axis. U_0 and U_1 are indifference curves, each showing combinations of wage and pension benefits that yield a given level of utility.

If the employer is willing to spend a total of m_1 dollars in compensating the worker with wage and pension benefits and is willing to exchange wages for pensions at a rate of (c_w/c_r), then the employer will offer the worker any combination of wages and pensions that lies along the locus:

$$z_w c_w + z_r c_r = m_1. \qquad (2.3)$$

Note that c_w is the employer's cost of providing wages, and c_r is the employer's cost of providing pensions. Note also that the dollar amount m_1 equals total compensation (m) minus the predetermined expenditure on health insurance.

Figure 2.1. **The optimal mix of wages and pension benefits shifts from (z_w^*, z_r^*) without income taxation to (z_w^{**}, z_r^{**}) with an income tax. z_w denotes the quantity of wages, z_r denotes the quantity of pension benefits.**

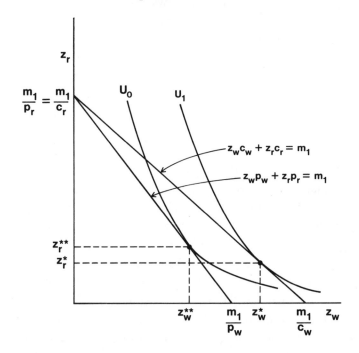

Given this initial budget constraint, the worker would maximize utility by choosing a quantity of wages, z_w^*, and a quantity of pensions, z_r^*, as shown in figure 2.1.

The initial constraint described by equation (2.3), however, is not the constraint that the worker finally faces. Under the current tax system, the worker's wages would be taxed at some marginal rate (t) whereas the employer's contributions to the worker's pension benefits would go untaxed. It follows that the budget constraint facing the worker pivots to

$$z_w p_w + z_r p_r = m_1 \qquad (2.4)$$

and the worker maximizes utility subject to this tax-modified constraint. The new optimal bundle of wages and pensions is given by (z_w^{**}, z_r^{**}).

Note that (p_w/p_r) is the rate at which the worker is able to exchange wages for pensions; that is, p_w and p_r are the tax-modified prices of wages and pensions. The relation between (p_w/p_r), which is the rate at which the worker is able to exchange wages for pensions, and (c_w/c_r), which is the rate at which the employer is willing to trade wages for pensions, is a function of the marginal tax rate:

$$p_w/p_r=(c_w/c_r)/(1-t). \qquad (2.5)$$

If $c_w=c_r$, equation (2.5) can be simplified to:

$$p_w/p_r=1/(1-t). \qquad (2.6)$$

An important simplification that has been incorporated into figure 2.1 is that the marginal tax rate (t) is taken as constant. In fact, of course, the marginal tax rate facing a worker varies with the income of the worker and his or her spouse. This variation in the marginal tax rate is both a blessing and a bane. It is a blessing because variation in t means that we will observe variation in the price ratio (p_w/p_r) facing different individuals or groups in any sample where there is variation in taxable income. Such variation will be central to estimating some representation of the utility function (eq. 2.1). Further, because marginal tax rates are a discontinuous function (or step function) of income, it should be possible to separate the effects of changes in income from the effects of changes in the relative price of wages and pensions. That is, income and the price ratio do vary independently; hence, econometric estimation of both substitution effects (which could also be thought of as tax effects) and income effects should be possible.

The variation of the marginal tax rate with income is a bane because this variation makes the budget constraint facing the worker nonlinear, rather than linear as shown in figure 2.1. That is, as the share of total compensation received as wages increases, the marginal tax rate will increase. In figure 2.1, the budget constraint labeled $z_w p_w+z_r p_r=m_1$ should bend toward the wage axis and intercept the wage axis at some point to the left of m_1/p_w. The nonlinearity of the budget constraint has econometric implications that are discussed below.

Figure 2.2. Relative cost to employers of pension and health insurance provision and the optimal mix of pension and health insurance benefits. The optimal mix of pension benefits shifts from (z_r^*, z_h^*) under the initial relative cost (to employers) of pensions and health insurance to (z_r^{**}, z_h^{**}) when the cost of pensions falls relative to health insurance.

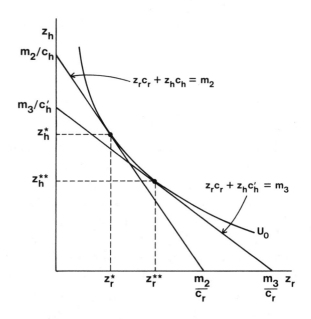

Fringe Benefit Costs and the Tradeoff Between Pensions and Health Insurance

Suppose now that the quantity of *wage* benefits has been predetermined and is held fixed, so that we may show the tradeoff between pensions and health insurance benefits in a two-dimensional graph. Figure 2.2 is such a graph; it shows the representative worker's preferences, this time for pension benefits (z_r, shown on the horizontal axis) and health insurance benefits (z_h, shown on the vertical axis). The indifference curve U_0 shows combinations of pension and health insurance benefits that give the worker equal satisfaction.

The key to analyzing substitution between pensions and health insurance benefits is to note that the employer's cost of providing pensions differs from the cost of providing health benefits. If the employer is willing to spend a total of m_2 dollars in compensating this worker with pensions and health insurance, and if the firm must pay c_r per unit of pension benefit, and c_h per unit of health insurance, then the firm will offer this worker any combination of pensions and health benefits lying on the locus:

$$z_r c_r + z_h c_h = m_2. \tag{2.7}$$

The dollar amount m_2 equals total compensation (m) minus the predetermined expenditure on wages. The dollar expenditures on pensions and health benefits are the two terms on the left-hand side of equation (2.7).

In the absence of any taxes on either fringe benefit, the worker will choose the fringe benefit package (z_r^*, z_h^*). A different employer, however, might face different costs of providing pensions and health benefits. For example, a small employer might face higher per unit insurance costs than a large employer (so that the cost of health benefits now equals c_h'), and might be willing to make a total dollar expenditure on pensions and health insurance equal to m_3, which would yield the set of pension-health offerings depicted by $z_r c_r + z_h c_h' = m_3$. In this latter case, the worker chooses a different fringe benefit package (z_r^{**}, z_h^{**}), with more pension benefits and less health insurance.[6] Note also that if a given employer faced rising health insurance costs over time, the initial constraint would pivot, and a similar substitution of pensions for health benefits would be likely to result.

A More Formal Statement of the Model

Recall our basic supposition that the worker's utility depends on the *quantities* of wage benefits (z_w), pensions or retirement benefits (z_r), and health insurance benefits (z_h):

$$U = U(z_w, z_r, z_h). \tag{2.1}$$

Empirical estimates of this utility function would yield information about how substitutable are these three components of compensation for one another. Such information could, in turn, be used to estimate how a change in tax policy that favored one component of compensation would affect demand for all three components of compensation. In effect, we are trying to estimate the shapes of the indifference curves shown in figures 2.1 and 2.2, and to use those estimates to predict how much substitution of one form of compensation for another would occur in response to a shift of the budget constraint.

Elasticities to Be Estimated

More precisely, we seek estimates of the following elasticities:

1. *The Uncompensated Own- and Cross-Price Elasticities of Demand for Benefit i:*

$$\eta_{ij} = (\partial z_i / \partial p_j)(p_j / z_i). \tag{2.8}$$

This is the percentage change in demand for benefit i that can be expected in response to a 1 percent change in the price of benefit j. η_{ij} is often referred to as the Marshallian price elasticity of demand.

2. *The Compensated Own- and Cross-Price Elasticities of Demand for Benefit i:*

$$\eta_{ij}^* = (\partial z_i / \partial p_j)_{\bar{U}}(p_j / z_i). \tag{2.9}$$

This is the percentage change in demand for benefit i that can be expected in response to a 1 percent change in the price of benefit j, holding utility constant. That is, η_{ij}^* measures changes in demand that take place after the worker has been compensated for any changes in utility that occur as a result of the price change. η_{ij}^* is often referred to as the Hicksian compensated elasticity of demand.

3. *The Income Elasticity of Demand for Benefit i:*

$$\eta_{im} = (\partial z_i / \partial m)(m/z_i). \qquad (2.10)$$

This is the percentage change in demand for benefit i that occurs in response to a 1 percent change in total compensation.

4. *The Elasticity of Substitution between Benefit i and Benefit j:*

$$\sigma_{ij} = \eta_{ij}^* / s_j \qquad (2.11)$$

where s_j is the share of total compensation received as benefit j. This is a measure of the strength and type of relationship (substitutability or complementarity) between benefits i and j. It can be either positive or negative. If σ_{ij} is positive, the benefits are substitutes; if negative, they are complements.

These four elasticities are tied together by the Slutsky relation, which in elasticity form can be written:

$$\eta_{ij} = \eta_{ij}^* - s_j \eta_{im} \qquad (2.12)$$

or, by substituting equation (2.11) into equation (2.12),

$$\eta_{ij} = \sigma_{ij} s_j - s_j \eta_{im}. \qquad (2.13)$$

Estimates of these elasticities will provide the information that is needed to predict the effects of various tax changes on the demand for each form of compensation.

A System of Demand Equations
for the Components of Compensation

Our goal, then, is to estimate some representation of the utility function (eq. 2.1), so as to obtain an unrestricted set of price, income, and substitution elasticities as defined by equations (2.8) through (2.11) above. The problem is that utility (U) is unobservable, so that a utility function such as equation (2.1) cannot be estimated directly. The most straightforward way of solving this problem is to manipulate or transform the direct utility function into a form that permits estimation and yields the same information about demand and substitution possibilities. Duality theory allows one to make just such manipulations. It turns out that if the direct utility function (eq. 2.1) is well-behaved, then an *indirect utility function*, dual to it, can be written showing the maximum utility attainable by a worker facing a price of wage benefits (p_w), a price of retirement benefits (p_r), a price of health benefits (p_h), and a given level of total compensation (m):

$$V = V(p_w, p_r, p_h, m). \tag{2.14}$$

Further, the indirect utility function may be solved for the minimum expenditure or cost (C) required to attain a specified level of utility (U), given prices (p_w, p_r, and p_h). So rewritten, equation (2.14) becomes a *consumer cost function* (or *expenditure function*):

$$C = C(p_w, p_r, p_h, U). \tag{2.15}$$

Since our goal is to estimate an unrestricted set of elasticities of substitution for wages, pension benefits, and health benefits, it is desirable to estimate an arbitrary approximation to either the indirect utility function (eq. 2.14) or the consumer cost function (eq. 2.15) set out above. For example, a translog approximation to the indirect utility function could be estimated, as it has been in earlier work on similar issues (Woodbury 1983, 1985a). Although satisfactory, the translog indirect utility function requires costly nonlinear estimation techniques unless one is willing to restrict income elasticities to unity and estimate a homothetic indirect utility function. Since we do not wish to impose unitary income elasticities, it would be advantageous to find some alternative.

One attractive alternative is to estimate a representation of the consumer cost function represented by equation (2.15). Deaton and Muellbauer (1980a) have developed a flexible approximation to the consumer cost function that results in an easily estimated system of consumer demand equations. They start with a representation of the consumer cost function known as the PIGLOG class (for Price Independent Generalized Linear Logarithmic). For the case of three goods (w,

r, and h), Deaton and Muellbauer's consumer cost function can be written as:

$$ln\ C(p_w, p_r, p_h, U) = \tag{2.16}$$
$$a_0 + a'_w ln\ p_w + a'_r ln\ p_r + a'_h ln\ p_h +$$
$$(\tfrac{1}{2})b'_{ww}(ln\ p_w)^2 + (\tfrac{1}{2})b'_{wr}(ln\ p_w)(ln\ p_r) +$$
$$(\tfrac{1}{2})b'_{wh}(ln\ p_w)(ln\ p_h) +$$
$$(\tfrac{1}{2})b'_{rw}(ln\ p_r)(ln\ p_w) + (\tfrac{1}{2})b'_{rr}(ln\ p_r)^2 +$$
$$(\tfrac{1}{2})b'_{rh}(ln\ p_r)(ln\ p_h) +$$
$$(\tfrac{1}{2})b'_{hw}(ln\ p_h)(ln\ p_w) + (\tfrac{1}{2})b'_{hr}(ln\ p_h)(ln\ p_r) +$$
$$(\tfrac{1}{2})b'_{hh}(ln\ p_h)^2 + Ub_0(p_w)^{b_w}(p_r)^{b_r}(p_h)^{b_h}.$$

All variables in equation (2.16) have been defined previously, except for the parameters a_0, a'_i, b'_{ij}, b_0, and b_i. These parameters characterize preferences for the various forms of compensation and will be estimated econometrically. The parameter estimates in turn allow one to compute directly the price, income, and substitution elasticities set out in equations (2.8) through (2.11). (See below.)

Demand functions for wage benefits, pensions, and health insurance can be derived from equation (2.16) by differentiating with respect to p_w, p_r, and p_h. This is the well-known property of cost functions developed by Shephard (1970). By some further manipulation, each demand function can be transformed into a demand function in budget-share form. For the consumer cost function represented by equation (2.16), these budget shares are:

$$s_w = a'_w + b_{ww} ln\ p_w + b_{wr} ln\ p_r + b_{wh} ln\ p_h \tag{2.17}$$
$$+ b_w ln(m/P)$$

$$s_r = a'_r + b_{rw} ln\ p_w + b_{rr} ln\ p_r + b_{rh} ln\ p_h \tag{2.18}$$
$$+ b_r ln(m/P)$$

$$s_h = a'_h + b_{hw} ln\ p_w + b_{hr} ln\ p_r + b_{hh} ln\ p_h \tag{2.19}$$
$$+ b_h ln(m/P)$$

where $b_{ij} = (\tfrac{1}{2})(b'_{ij} + b'_{ji})$.

Equations (2.17), (2.18), and (2.19) are three expenditure share equations. They say that the share of total compensation received in each form is a function of prices and an income term (m/P). Specifically, s_w is the share of compensation received as wages, s_r is the share received as pension or retirement benefits, and s_h is the share received as health benefits. The price of wages (p_w), the price of pension or retirement benefits (p_r), and the price of health benefits (p_h) are as defined earlier. The income term (m/P) equals after-tax total compensation (m) divided by a price index, P.

There is an exact definition of P (Deaton and Muellbauer 1980a, p. 314), which leads to a specification requiring nonlinear estimation techniques. Because nonlinear techniques are expensive and unattractive, several researchers, including Deaton and Muellbauer, have approximated P as:

$$ln\ P^* = s_w ln\ p_w + s_r ln\ p_r + s_h ln\ p_h \qquad (2.20)$$

where P^* is the approximation to P. Using this approximation is attractive because it turns P into a predetermined variable, and hence gives us a model that is linear in parameters and relatively simple to estimate. Also, those who have used it (Deaton and Muellbauer 1980a; Anderson and Blundell 1983, 1984; and Kang 1983) have found P^* to be a good approximation to the exact definition of P. Accordingly, the approximation will be used throughout this work.

Implementing the Model

Deaton and Muellbauer call the demand system represented by equations (2.17) through (2.19) the Almost Ideal Demand System (or, rather inauspiciously, the "AIDS") because it is log-linear in prices and income once an approximation to P has been selected. Linearity makes the Deaton-Muellbauer system simpler to estimate than other flexible representations of consumer preferences, such as the translog or generalized Leontief. Indeed, linearity is the most significant advantage of the Deaton-Muellbauer demand system over other demand systems that are consistent with consumer theory and allow estimation of an unrestricted set of price, income, and substitution elasticities.

Adding Demographic and Other Variables to the Model

An additional advantage of the Deaton-Muellbauer system is that it easily accommodates variables other than prices and income that may influence the observed share of fringe benefits. To this point in the discussion, there has been no attempt to include such variables. But there can be little doubt that unbiased estimation of the demand elasticities of interest requires that we control for variables such as individual demographic characteristics.

How to include demographic and other variables in empirical demand analysis is a problem that has been the topic of considerable research (see, for example, Lau, Lin, and Yotopoulos 1978; Pollak and Wales 1981; and Lewbel 1985). The solution adopted here is the obvious one in the context of the Deaton-Muellbauer demand system. Since each budget share includes a constant term, it is natural to suppose that the constant shifts with demographic changes. If we make such an assumption, which is known as demographic budget share translation, then equations (2.17) through (2.19) can be rewritten as follows:

$$s_w = a_w + b_{ww} ln\, p_w + b_{wr} ln\, p_r + b_{wh} ln\, p_h + b_w ln(m/P^*) + \quad (2.21)$$
$$d_{w1} x_1 + \ldots + d_{wK} x_K$$

$$s_r = a_r + b_{rw} ln\, p_w + b_{rr} ln\, p_r + b_{rh} ln\, p_h + b_r ln(m/P^*) + \quad (2.22)$$
$$d_{w1} x_1 + \ldots + d_{wK} x_K$$

$$s_h = a_h + b_{hw} ln\, p_w + b_{hr} ln\, p_r + b_{hh} ln\, p_h + b_h ln(m/P^*) + \quad (2.23)$$
$$d_{w1} x_1 + \ldots + d_{wK} x_K.$$

In equations (2.21) through (2.23), $x_1, \ldots, x_K$ represent the demographic (and other) variables that shift the budget shares, and the d_{ik} are coefficients representing the effects of changes in those variables on the shares. Also, the approximation P^* has been substituted for P. Note that use of P^* results in a redefinition of the intercept terms (a_i) in equations (2.21) through (2.23), which equal $a_i' - b_i(ln\, g)$, where g is a scalar indicating how well P^* approximates P (if $g = 1$, the approximation is exact). (For details, see Deaton and Muellbauer 1980a, p. 316.)

Restrictions of Consumer Theory and Stochastic Assumptions

It is desirable for the demand system represented by equations (2.21) through (2.23) to exhibit three properties that are implied by consumer theory. These are usually referred to as the adding-up, homogeneity, and symmetry properties, and are treated in turn.

Adding-up simply means that the shares of the budget spent on the components of compensation sum to one. In order to satisfy the adding-up property, the system represented by equations (2.21) through (2.23) must satisfy the following across-equation constraints:

$$a_w + a_r + a_h = 1 \qquad (2.24)$$

$$b_{ww} + b_{rw} + b_{hw} = 0 \qquad (2.25)$$

$$b_{wr} + b_{rr} + b_{hr} = 0 \qquad (2.26)$$

$$b_{wh} + b_{rh} + b_{hh} = 0 \qquad (2.27)$$

$$b_w + b_r + b_h = 0 \qquad (2.28)$$

$$d_{wk} + d_{rk} + d_{hk} = 0 \text{ for all } k. \qquad (2.29)$$

In practice, the adding-up constraint is imposed by constructing the data so that the budget shares sum to one for each observation, and so that the mean of each price and income variable is unity (hence the natural logarithm of each mean is zero). Since, as discussed presently, only two of the three share equations must be estimated, constructing the budget shares in this way will cause the adding-up restrictions to be satisfied automatically.

Homogeneity implies that a doubling of both prices and income would leave the demand for each component of compensation unchanged. For the system to be homogeneous (specifically, homogeneous of degree zero in prices and income), the following within-equation constraints must be imposed:

$$b_{ww} + b_{wr} + b_{wh} = 0 \qquad (2.30)$$

$$b_{rw} + b_{rr} + b_{rh} = 0 \qquad (2.31)$$

$$b_{hw}+b_{hr}+b_{hh}=0. \qquad (2.32)$$

Finally, symmetry means that the cross-substitution effects must be symmetric — that is, $\sigma_{ij}=\sigma_{ji}$. Such symmetry can be imposed by constraining b_{ij} to equal b_{ji} across equations in the econometric estimation.

If we impose the adding-up, homogeneity, and symmetry constraints on equations (2.21) through (2.23), and append a random disturbance term to each, we obtain the following three share equations:

$$s_w=a_w+b_{wr}ln(p_r/p_w)+b_{wh}ln(p_h/p_w)+b_wln(m/P^*)+ \qquad (2.33)$$
$$d_{w1}x_1+\ldots+d_{wK}x_K+u_w$$

$$s_r=a_r+b_{rr}ln(p_r/p_w)+b_{rh}ln(p_h/p_w)+b_rln(m/P^*)+ \qquad (2.34)$$
$$d_{r1}x_1+\ldots+d_{rK}x_K+u_r$$

$$s_h=a_h+b_{rh}ln(p_r/p_w)+b_{hh}ln(p_h/p_w)+b_hln(m/P^*)+ \qquad (2.35)$$
$$d_{h1}x_1+\ldots+d_{hK}x_K+u_h$$

where the random disturbance terms — u_w, u_r, and u_h — are assumed to be normally distributed with zero mean.

Two points are worth noting. First, the price ratios used in equations (2.33) through (2.35) are the inverses of those stated as equations (2.5) and (2.6). This poses no problem — equations (2.5) and (2.6) simply define the inverses of the appropriate price ratios. Second, because the shares (s_w, s_r, and s_h) sum to one, only two of the above three equations are independent. As a result, estimation of equations (2.33) through (2.35) can be accomplished by arbitrarily deleting one of the three equations and performing an iterative version of Zellner's seemingly unrelated regression procedure on the remaining two. (See Christensen and Manser 1976, 1977 for further discussion and references.) Results will be the same regardless of which equation is deleted, and will be maximum likelihood estimates.

Prices of the Components of Compensation

The demand system given by equations (2.33) through (2.35) is driven by variation in the relative prices of the components of compensation $[(p_r/p_w)$ and $(p_h/p_w)]$, and by variation in income (m/P^*). As a result, it is important to understand the origin of these price ratios and the income term. A complete treatment of the construction of these variables can be given only in the context of the data being considered, but the following general points are in order.

Recall that the price of wage benefits relative to the price of pensions is:

$$p_w/p_r = (c_w/c_r)/(1-t) \qquad (2.5)$$

where c_w is the employer's cost of wage benefits, c_r is the employer's cost of pension benefits, and t is the marginal tax rate on wages faced by the worker. That is, income taxation shifts the rate at which the worker can trade wages for pensions, since the worker's wages are taxed at some marginal rate (t) but the employer's contributions to pensions are untaxed. Hence, wages have become more expensive relative to pensions as a result of income taxation.

Because the employer's contributions to health insurance are also untaxed, income taxation will shift the rate at which the worker can trade wages for health insurance benefits:

$$p_w/p_h = (c_w/c_h)/(1-t) \qquad (2.36)$$

where c_h is the employer's cost of providing health insurance benefits.

Finally, income taxation will not affect the tradeoff between pensions and health benefits faced by the worker if all fringe benefits are untaxed. That is,

$$p_r/p_h = c_r/c_h \qquad (2.37)$$

or the rate at which the worker can ultimately trade health for retirement benefits is the same as the rate at which the employer can trade them.

Note that only two of the three price ratios represented by equations (2.5), (2.36), and (2.37) are independent. This is another way of seeing that only two of the three equations of the demand system must be estimated. Indeed, the only relative prices needed to estimate the demand system represented by equations (2.33) through (2.35) are (p_w/p_r) and (p_w/p_h).

How are the needed price ratios (p_w/p_r) and (p_w/p_h) to be obtained? If we are willing to assume that the cost of pensions relative to the cost of wages — that is, c_w/c_r — equals an arbitrary constant, then the price ratio (p_w/p_r) can be written simply as:

$$p_w/p_r = k/(1-t) \qquad (2.6a)$$

where k is the constant of proportionality between wage and pension costs. Since the only source of variation in (p_w/p_r) is the marginal tax rate (t) it is harmless to set c equal to 1 and to compute:

$$p_w/p_r = 1/(1-t). \qquad (2.6)$$

Hence, (p_w/p_r) is computed as a simple transformation of the marginal tax rate. (We explain how measures of the marginal tax rate are obtained in the next chapter.)

It is possible that the ratio of wage to pension costs (k) is *not* constant, but varies from industry to industry. The source of this variation can be thought of as exogenous interindustry differences in the organization of production, which lead to differing specific human capital requirements, turnover of workers, and pension provision. In our empirical specifications in the next chapter, we include proxies for the organization of production independently, rather than attempting to embed the effects of differing organization of production in the price ratio (p_w/p_r). The first reason for this independent inclusion is its feasibility and the apparent infeasibility of embedding the effect of differences in the organization of production in the price ratio (p_w/p_r).

The second reason is that independent inclusion of a specific human capital measure offers a way of testing for so-called agency incentives for pension provision. As Lazear (1981), Mumy and Manson (1985), and Bell and Hart (1990) have pointed out, firms may offer deferred compensation as an inducement to their employees to work hard and remain with the firm over many years, since only employees who stay with the firm will receive their deferred compensation. It follows that deferred compensation such as pensions will be important in industries where the organization of production places a premium on skill and specific human capital. Accordingly, we include proxies for specific human capital in our estimates of fringe benefit demand reported in the next chapter, with the expectation that higher levels of specific human capital will be related to a higher proportion of total compensation received as pensions, but will be unrelated to the share of compensation received as health insurance.[7]

Estimates of (p_w/p_h) can be obtained by observing health insurance costs, which can be observed both over time and from employer to employer. Changes over time may be obtained from the price index of health insurance reported in the National Income and Product Accounts (U.S. Department of Commerce, Bureau of Economic Analysis 1986, Table 7.10). Differences from employer to employer are more difficult to measure. Health insurance carriers vary their rates depending on the health and medical care experience of a group, which in turn depends on the group's size, occupational mix, and demographic composition. Estimation of these variations is taken up in the next chapter.

To summarize, since variation in the price of wage benefits relative to pension and health benefits can be observed, it should be possible to estimate tradeoffs between wages and pensions, between wages and health insurance, and between pensions and health insurance. The tradeoff between pensions and health insurance is of special interest. First, it has not been estimated in previous research. Moreover, proposals have been advanced to tax health insurance contributions but not pension contributions under the federal personal income tax. Determining the effect of such a tax policy on pension provision requires understanding of the possibilities for substituting pensions for health insurance. The assumption made in all previous analyses of the provision of fringe benefits has been that employers' costs of providing a unit of each benefit $(c_w, c_r, \text{and } c_h)$ are equal. Only by relaxing this assumption can we consider tradeoffs within the fringe benefit package, such as the tradeoff between pensions and health insurance.

Progressive Taxes and Nonlinearity of the Budget Constraint

Recall that because the marginal tax rate facing a worker increases as his or her income increases, the tradeoff between wages and fringe benefits facing that worker will be nonlinear. That is, the lower of the two budget constraints in figure 2.1 should actually bend toward the wage axis as the worker consumes more wages and fewer fringe benefits.

In fact, the nonlinearity of the budget constraint in the context of fringe benefit demand is a special case of a more general problem that results from progressive taxation. For example, the budget constraint facing workers when they make their labor supply decision is also nonlinear, because as a worker's hours of work increase, the marginal tax rate increases and the worker's net after-tax wage declines. The traditional way of handling this problem (Hall 1973; Wales 1973) is to use a linear approximation to the nonlinear budget constraint by, in effect, drawing a straight line, tangent to the indifference curve representing maximum attainable utility, through each individual's observed consumption bundle.

The linear approximation approach is illustrated in figure 2.3, which is a redrawing of figure 2.1 that has been corrected for the presence of progressive taxation. Three budget constraints are shown in figure 2.3. The first is the budget constraint in the absence of any income tax, which is repeated from figure 2.1. The second is the nonlinear budget constraint faced by a worker under progressive taxation. Again, this budget constraint curves toward the wage axis as the share of wages in total compensation increases. The third is the "linearized" budget constraint, which is a straight line tangent to the actual constraint at the optimal bundle of pensions and wages (z_w^{**}, z_r^{**}).

The linear approximation approach entails assigning price and income data to each observation as follows. First, the slope of the linearized constraint is taken as the price of wages relative to pensions (p_w/p_r). Second, the wage intercept of the linearized constraint (z_w^0 in figure 2.3) multiplied by the price of wages (p_w) is taken as total compensation. Equivalently, the observed marginal tax rate is assigned to each observation in the sample, and the sum of observed after-tax wages, pension contributions, and health insurance contributions is assigned to each observation as total compensation.

The problem posed by the linear approximation method is econo-

Figure 2.3. Progressive income taxation, the nonlinear budget
constraint, and the linear approximation method.

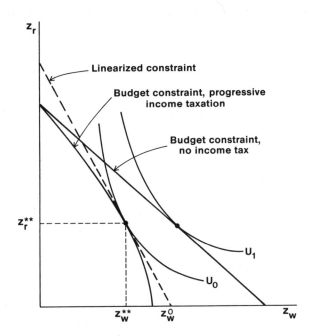

metric: the marginal tax rate observed for each worker (or the price of
wages relative to pensions based on that tax rate) is no longer exogenous
under progressive income taxation. The marginal tax rate is, in effect,
chosen by the worker, as is easily seen from figure 2.3. The worker
depicted in the figure has chosen the compensation bundle (z_w^{**}, z_r^{**}), and
hence faces the marginal tax rate given by the slope of the dashed line.
But another worker with different preferences might choose a different
compensation bundle – that is, a different point on the curved budget
constraint – and would as a result face a different marginal tax rate.
Hence, the marginal tax rate is chosen along with the compensation
bundle, and is endogenous. In the worst case, using the observed
marginal tax rate (or relative prices derived from it) as an independent
variable could lead to inconsistent estimates of the effect of changes in
the marginal tax rate on whatever dependent variable is of interest.

A maximum likelihood solution to the problem of nonlinear budget constraints has been suggested and implemented by Burtless and Hausman (1978) and Wales and Woodland (1979). (See also Hausman 1985; Moffitt 1986, 1990; and Megdal 1987.) For two reasons, we have not used the maximum likelihood solution to the problem posed by the nonlinear budget constraint. First, the estimation procedure used is already complex and expensive, and handling the nonlinear budget constraint by maximum likelihood would make it more so. Second, it appears that the linear approximation method we use tends to underestimate "true" elasticities of substitution estimated by maximum likelihood.[8] Hence, even though the elasticities of substitution estimated in the next chapter tend to be large, it is perhaps best to view them as lower-bound estimates of the true elasticities of substitution between various components of compensation.

Computation of Elasticities

We asserted above that estimates of the parameters of the demand system would yield, in turn, estimates of the price, income, and substitution elasticities that are needed to predict the effects of various tax changes on the demand for fringe benefits. (The elasticities were written out in equations (2.8) through (2.11).)

The formulas used to compute each elasticity from the parameters of the Deaton-Muellbauer demand system, written as equations (2.33) through (2.35), are as follows.[9] Start with the uncompensated price elasticities (eq. 2.8). The uncompensated own-price elasticities of demand for benefit i can be computed as:

$$\eta_{ii} = (\partial z_i / \partial p_i)(p_i / z_i) = (b_{ii}/s_i) - b_i - 1. \qquad (2.8a)$$

The uncompensated $cross$-price elasticities are:

$$\eta_{ij} = (\partial z_i / \partial p_j)(p_j / z_i) = (b_{ij}/s_i) - b_i(s_j/s_i). \qquad (2.8b)$$

The $compensated$ own- and cross-price elasticities can be computed as:

$$\eta_{ii}^* = (\partial z_i / \partial p_i)_{\bar{U}} (p_i / z_i) = (b_{ii} / s_i) + s_i - 1 \qquad (2.9a)$$

and

$$\eta_{ij}^* = (\partial z_i / \partial p_j)_{\bar{U}} (p_j / z_i) = (b_{ij} / s_i) + s_j. \qquad (2.9b)$$

Next, the income elasticities can be computed as:

$$\eta_{im} = (\partial z_i / \partial m)(m / z_i) = (b_i / s_i) + 1. \qquad (2.10a)$$

Finally, the elasticities of substitution are:

$$\sigma_{ii} = \eta_{ii}^* / s_i = (b_{ii} / s_i^2) - (1 / s_i) + 1 \qquad (2.11a)$$

and

$$\sigma_{ij} = \eta_{ij}^* / s_j = (b_{ij} / s_i s_j) + 1. \qquad (2.11b)$$

In equations (2.8a) through (2.11b), the required parameters (b_i, b_{ij}) and shares (s_i) are from equations (2.33) through (2.35).

Confidence Intervals for the Elasticities

Estimating the price, income, and substitution elasticities set out above is the main objective of the empirical work presented in the next chapter. Because these elasticities are central to an understanding of how tax policy changes might affect the mix of total compensation, it would be highly desirable to construct confidence intervals around each elasticity estimate, so that statistical tests of significance could be performed.

Constructing confidence intervals around the elasticities estimated using the Deaton-Muellbauer and other flexible demand systems poses a well-known problem that has been discussed by many users of flexible functional forms (Anderson and Thursby 1986; Krinsky and Robb 1986; Grant and Hamermesh 1981; Toevs 1980, 1982). It is clear from the elasticity formulas presented above that each elasticity is a nonlinear function of parameters and compensation shares. As a result, it is not obvious what measure of error should be associated with these elasticity estimates.

One possible measure of the error associated with each elasticity is the asymptotic variance (and covariances) of the estimated parameter (or parameters) underlying the elasticity in question. This is easy to calculate in cases where only one parameter is used to compute an elasticity. In other cases, this solution involves computing the variance of a linear combination of parameters. This is true, for example, in the case of the uncompensated elasticities, since both b_i and either b_{ii} or b_{ij} underlie these.[10]

A remaining problem with this measure of error associated with the computed elasticities is that it treats only the parameters (b_i, b_{ii}, and b_{ij}) as stochastic; the compensation shares (s_i) are assumed nonstochastic. A case can be made that the shares should in fact be treated as random variables. Accordingly, an improved measure of error associated with the elasticities would be the variance of each elasticity derived by taking a Taylor expansion of each elasticity around the sample mean, which includes variances and covariances of shares, as well as variances and covariances of parameters (see, for example, Kmenta 1986, p. 486). Standard errors based on variances computed in this way are reported in tables 3.3 and 3.6 in chapter 3.

Restatement of the Model

The model of fringe benefit provision developed in this chapter is based on the following "story." The employer offers a menu of compensation packages to workers, who select the package that maximizes their well-being. The menu offered by employers implies certain tradeoffs between components of compensation that the employer is willing to make, and these tradeoffs depend in turn on the employer's cost of providing each benefit. The package that workers choose from the menu depends on their preferences (which depend in part on characteristics such as age and marital status), on their level of total compensation, and on the prices of the components of compensation. The prices facing workers depend not only on the employer's costs of providing each component of the package, but also on the differential tax treatment of each component.[11]

This story can be formalized, and a model that can be estimated econometrically can be derived. We follow Deaton and Muellbauer (1980a) and specify an expenditure function in flexible form. From this flexible expenditure function, the following system of demand equations for wages, pensions, and health insurance benefits can be derived:

$$s_w = a_w + b_{wr}ln(p_r/p_w) + b_{wh}ln(p_h/p_w) + b_w ln(m/P^*) + \quad (2.33)$$
$$d_{w1}x_1 + \ldots + d_{wK}x_K + u_w$$

$$s_r = a_r + b_{rr}ln(p_r/p_w) + b_{rh}ln(p_h/p_w) + b_r ln(m/P^*) + \quad (2.34)$$
$$d_{r1}x_1 + \ldots + d_{rK}x_K + u_r$$

$$s_h = a_h + b_{rh}ln(p_r/p_w) + b_{hh}ln(p_h/p_w) + b_h ln(m/P^*) + \quad (2.35)$$
$$d_{h1}x_1 + \ldots + d_{hK}x_K + u_h.$$

This is a standard set of demand equations, in the sense that the demand for each component of compensation is modeled as a function of the prices of those benefits, income, and other characteristics such as age and sex. In these equations, s_w, s_r, and s_h are the shares (or proportions) of total compensation received in the form of wages, pension contributions, and health insurance benefits; (p_r/p_w) and (p_h/p_w) are the prices of pensions and health insurance, relative to wages, that face workers; m is total compensation in dollars; P^* is a price index approximated by $ln\ P^* = s_w ln\ p_w + s_r ln\ p_r + s_h ln\ p_h$; x_1 through x_K are control variables other than prices and income, such as demographic characteristics, that might affect the demand for fringe benefits; and u_w, u_r, and u_h, are random disturbance terms that are assumed to be normally distributed with zero mean.

The a_i, b_{ij}, b_i, and d_{ik} are parameters to be estimated. These parameters can be interpreted as follows. The b_{ij} parameters show the effect of changes in relative prices on the budget shares, holding real income constant. More precisely, a 1 percent increase in the price of component i changes the share of component j by $(b_{ij}/100)$, other things equal. The b_i parameters show the effect of changes in real total compensation on compensation shares. For a component of compensation that is a luxury,

b_i will be positive; for a component that is a necessity, b_i will be negative.[12] In addition, estimates of the b_{ij} and b_i parameters yield in turn estimates of the price, income, and substitution elasticities that are needed to determine the effect of changing tax policy on the provision of the different forms of fringe benefits. Finally, the d_{ik} show the influence of the demographic and other characteristics on each compensation share. A unit increase in any of these other control variables will change the compensation share in question by d_{ik}, all else equal.

Two final points deserve emphasis. First, the relative prices in the demand system are constructed with an eye to both the employer's cost of providing each component of compensation, and to the tax treatment of each component. Specifically, the relative prices are defined by:

$$p_w/p_r = (c_w/c_r)/(1-t) \tag{2.5}$$

and

$$p_w/p_h = (c_w/c_h)/(1-t) \tag{2.36}$$

where c_w, c_r, and c_h are the employer's cost of providing a unit of pension benefits, a unit of wage benefits, and a unit of health insurance benefits; and t is the marginal tax on income faced by the worker. Actual measurement of these relative prices is an important part of the work presented in the next chapter.[13] Second, earlier work on fringe benefits has examined only the choice between wages and fringe benefits taken as a whole. The demand system set out above specifies separate equations for pensions and health insurance, and hence allows examination of tradeoffs within the fringe benefit package. It is necessary to estimate only two of the three equations (2.33) through (2.35), because only two are independent. Although the choice of which equations to estimate is arbitrary, we estimate the two fringe benefit share equations [(2.34) and (2.35)] in the next chapter, because our main concern is with the influence of changing prices and incomes on fringe benefits.

Appendix to Chapter 2
Summary of Notation

a_i', a_i — Share equation intercept terms in the Deaton-Muellbauer Almost Ideal Demand System. Note that $a_i = a_i' - b_i(ln\ g)$. See below for definitions of b_i and g.

b_i — Parameters, showing the effect of changes in real total compensation on compensation shares, in the Deaton-Muellbauer Almost Ideal Demand System.

b_{ij}', b_{ij} — Parameters showing the influence of changes in relative prices on compensation shares in the Deaton-Muellbauer Almost Ideal Demand System. Note that $b_{ij} = (\frac{1}{2})(b_{ij}' + b_{ij}')$.

c_w, c_r, c_h — Cost to the employer of a unit of wage benefits, pension benefits, and health insurance benefits.

$C(.)$ — The consumer cost or expenditure function, indicating the minimum expenditure needed to attain a given level of utility (U) at a given set of benefit prices.

d_{ik} — Parameters showing the influence of the control variables $(x_1, \ldots, x_K)$ on compensation shares in the Deaton-Muellbauer Almost Ideal Demand System.

g — Scalar indicating the closeness of the approximation P^* to the true price index P.

m — Total compensation in dollars, exogenously set by the employer.

m' — Instrument for real total compensation used with the EEEC data in chapter 3. Equals average after-tax earnings of each worker group divided by the industry average share of compensation received as wages.

m_1 — Total compensation paid in wage and pension benefits (health insurance benefits predetermined).

m_2, m_3	Total compensation paid in pension and health insurance benefits (wage benefits predetermined).
p_w, p_r, p_h	Prices faced by workers of wage benefits, retirement benefits (referred to as pensions throughout the text), and health insurance benefits.
P	Aggregate price index of benefits.
P^*	Approximation to the aggregate price index used in the empirical work.
s_i	The share (proportion) of total compensation received as benefit i.
t	The marginal tax rate on income faced by the worker.
u_w, u_r, u_h	Random disturbance terms in the wage share, pension share, and health insurance share equations.
$U(.)$	The direct utility function, indicating the utility derived from consumption of a given bundle of benefit quantities.
$V(.)$	The indirect utility function, indicating the maximum utility attainable at a given set of benefit prices, and a given level of total compensation.
$x_1, \ldots, x_K$	Demographic, industry, and other control variables (other than prices and real total compensation) included in the benefit demand functions.
z_w, z_r, z_h	Quantities of wage benefits, retirement benefits (referred to as pensions throughout the text), and health insurance benefits. Optimal quantities are shown with asterisks.
η_{ii}, η_{ij}	The uncompensated own- and cross-price elasticities of demand for benefit i.
η_{im}	The income (or expenditure) elasticity of demand for benefit i.

η_{ii}^*, η_{ij}^* The compensated own- and cross-price elasticities of demand for benefit i.

σ_{ij} The elasticity of substitution between benefit i and benefit j. A positive σ_{ij} indicates that i and j are substitutes, a negative σ_{ij} indicates that they are complements.

NOTES

[1] It is true that employers may offer several types of health benefits and that pension benefits also may be somewhat flexible. Regarding health benefits, the variation may be in the delivery system—health maintenance organization, fee-for-service provider, or independent practice association. In some cases, the actual premiums charged will differ, as will the service provided. Hence, employees are allowed to choose, in some cases, from a limited menu of benefit packages offered by a given employer, in addition to having different menus offered by different employers.

[2] One can easily imagine a model of benefit determination that views the firm as providing a package of benefits that minimizes the firm's cost of retaining a workforce of given size and quality. But in such an approach, workers' responses to the tax treatment of benefits would be confounded with their underlying preferences for quantities of benefits.

[3] The limited experience rating of unemployment insurance and workers' compensation implies that firms do have some control over these legally mandated expenses. The difficulty economists have had in estimating a behavioral response of firms to experience rating, however, suggests that these expenses are largely beyond a firm's control.

[4] As already noted, we examine wages, pensions, and health insurance because they are the three largest components of total compensation that are provided voluntarily. Again, we omit fringe benefits that employers must provide by law—social security, unemployment insurance, and workers' compensation contributions, for example—because workers and employers have limited scope for choosing these. By omitting these so-called mandatory fringe benefits, the utility function (2.1) embodies the assumption that wages and voluntarily provided fringe b :fits are (as a group) weakly separable from all other goods that provide utility to workers. This assumption of weak separability implies that changes in the consumption of goods other than wages, pensions, and health benefits do not affect the marginal rate of substitution between, for example, wages and pensions. It would be useful to test empirically the assumption of separability, although no straightforward way of doing so suggests itself.

[5] The same points could be illustrated by fixing pension benefits and analyzing substitution between wages and health insurance, since for now we are assuming that wages are taxed and all fringe benefits are untaxed.

[6] Presumably, the two employers being considered would operate in different product and labor markets. Accordingly, total expenditures on pensions and health insurance could differ between the two employers without violating competitive assumptions. From an empirical standpoint, the key is to include appropriate controls for industry and workers' characteristics.

[7] Our approach is open to the criticism that pension provision and specific human capital are jointly determined; that is, causation does not run from specific human capital to pension provision, as our empirical specification would suggest.

[8] These are the results found by Wales and Woodland (1979). It is not obvious that their results can be generalized, but their case is similar to ours.

[9] Note that formulas (2.8a) through (2.11b) apply when the approximation to the price index (P^*) is used. Use of the approximation P^* results in elasticity formulas for the Deaton-Muellbauer demand system that differ from those that use the exact price index P – see, for example, Anderson and Blundell (1983).

[10] Consider for example, the variance of η_{ij}:

$$\begin{aligned} \text{var } (\eta_{ij}) &= \text{var}[(1/s_i)b_{ij} - (s_j/s_i)b_i] \\ &= [(1/s_i^2)\ \text{var}(b_{ij})] + [(s_j/s_i)^2\ \text{var } (b_i)] \\ &\quad - [2(s_j/s_i^2)\ \text{cov}(b_{ij},b_i)]. \end{aligned}$$

[11] Prices facing workers may in addition depend on the competitive position of the employer. That is, employers who possess market power may obtain rents by providing their employees with benefits obtained at favorable rates. We are grateful to William Alpert for this point.

[12] If η_{im} exceeds unity, then good i is a luxury, otherwise the good is a necessity. Referring to equation (2.10a), $\eta_{im} = (b_i/s_i) + 1$. Hence, η_{im} will always exceed unity if b_i is positive, but cannot exceed unity if b_i is negative. Also, if η_{im} is greater than zero, the good in question is normal; if η_{im} is negative it is inferior. To determine whether a component of compensation is normal or inferior, one needs to use (2.10a); in general, though, b_i must be negative and s_i must be small in order for η_{im} to be inferior.

[13] Note again that the price ratios in equations (2.5) and (2.36) define the inverses of those used in the estimating equations (2.33) through (2.35).

3

Estimates of the Demand for Fringe Benefits

Existing data on fringe benefits are notoriously imperfect, as many economists have pointed out (Antos 1983; Hamermesh 1983; Atrostic 1983; and Smith and Ehrenberg 1983, among others). One can imagine two kinds of data that would be ideal for examining the role of fringe benefits in the labor market. The first would be a broadly representative sample of individuals that would include complete information on the demographic and other characteristics of the workers in the sample (including age, marital status, employment status and earnings of spouse, family size, and so on), and a complete profile of each worker's nonwage benefit package. The second ideal data set would be a representative sample of establishments that would include a complete characterization of the establishment, the various groups of workers employed, and the fringe benefits provided to each of those groups. Alas, such ideal data sets are nonexistent.

Nevertheless, there exist at least two data bases that are serviceable for the purpose of estimating tradeoffs among various components of compensation. The first is a data set based on the unpublished two-digit industry data underlying the National Income and Product Accounts (NIPA) "other labor income" series for 1968 through 1982 (U.S. Department of Commerce, Bureau of Economic Analysis 1986). The second is a data base fashioned from the 1977 Survey of Employer Expenditures for Employee Compensation (hereafter, EEEC), the 1977 Current Population Survey, and the 1977–78 National Medical Care Expenditure Survey. In the first of these data sets, the unit of observation is the two-digit industry; in the second, it is the establishment. The advantage of using two separate data bases in exploring tradeoffs among wages, pension benefits, and health insurance benefits is that each data base has different strengths and weaknesses, and the results from one analysis can be used as a check on the other.[1]

This chapter offers two separate estimates of the demand for fringe benefits, the first using the NIPA data from 1968 to 1982, the second using the 1977 EEEC survey. In each case, the demand for pension benefits and the demand for health insurance benefits, as specified by equations (2.34) and (2.35) in the last chapter, are jointly estimated. Each set of estimates results in a complete set of price, income, and substitution elasticities. These estimates are of intrinsic interest, and will also be used to simulate the effects of tax policy changes in chapter 4.

It is useful to restate the equations to be estimated, so that the data requirements of the empirical work can be clearly understood. Recall from the last chapter that equations (2.33) through (2.35) model the demand for wages, pensions, and health insurance benefits. Because only two of the three equations are independent, we will estimate only the demand for pensions and health insurance:

$$s_r = a_r + b_{rr}ln(p_r/p_w) + b_{rh}ln(p_h/p_w) + b_r ln(m/P^*) + \quad (2.34)$$
$$d_{r1}x_1 + \ldots + d_{rK}x_K + u_r$$

$$s_h = a_h + b_{rh}ln(p_r/p_w) + b_{hh}ln(p_h/p_w) + b_h ln(m/P^*) + \quad (2.35)$$
$$d_{h1}x_1 + \ldots + d_{hK}x_K + u_h.$$

To repeat, this is a standard set of demand equations, in the sense that the demand for each component of compensation is modeled as a function of the relative prices of those benefits $[(p_r/p_w)$ and $(p_h/p_w)]$, real total compensation (m/P^*), and other characteristics such as age and sex $(x_1, \ldots, x_K)$. The dependent variables, s_r and s_h, are the shares (that is, proportions) of total compensation received in the form of pension contributions and health insurance benefits. The a_i, b_{ij}, b_i, and d_{ik} are parameters to be estimated, and u_r and u_h are random disturbances. (See chapter 2 for a complete development of the model, and the conclusion of that chapter for a summary.)

Prices and income drive any system of demand equations, and this demand system is no exception. All of the policy changes that will be simulated in the next chapter have their effect on the demand for fringe benefits and the mix of compensation through their effect on relative prices and income. It follows that construction of the relative price and income variables is of central importance. Recall from the last chapter the definition of the relative prices:[2]

$$p_w/p_r=(c_w/c_r)/(1-t), \text{ and} \tag{2.5}$$

$$p_w/p_h=(c_w/c_h)/(1-t), \tag{2.36}$$

where c_w, c_r, and c_h are the employer's cost of providing a unit of wage benefits, a unit of pension benefits, and a unit of health insurance benefits; and t is the marginal tax on income faced by the worker.

Four variables, c_w, c_r, c_h, and t, are needed to construct the above relative prices. How are these four variables to be observed? First, in using both the NIPA data and the EEEC survey, we will assume that the wage-pension cost ratio (c_w/c_r) is constant. As pointed out in the last chapter, this is a debatable assumption worth further research, but the problems to which it may give rise can be minimized by including a proxy for firm-specific human capital among the control variables ($x_1, \ldots, x_K$). Next, the wage health-insurance cost ratio (c_w/c_h) will be constructed from a hedonic model of the price of health insurance. This model is developed in the appendix to this chapter, and relies on the 1977–78 National Medical Care Expenditure Survey. The National Medical Care Expenditure Survey is a critical part of the empirical work presented in this chapter because it is the only existing data from which one can obtain measures of variation in health insurance costs from establishment to establishment and from industry to industry. The results of the hedonic model are applied to both the NIPA data and the EEEC survey.

Finally, the marginal tax rate (t) will be constructed from data on each observation in each sample. The methods involved in computing t for each of the two data sets will be discussed below, along with the development of each data set.

Estimates from the National Income and Product Accounts

Description of the Data

In the past 20 years, labor economists and other applied micro-economists have grown accustomed to using and interpreting household data, almost to the point where they distrust and eschew data in which the unit of observation is more highly aggregated than the household. Indeed, it is clear that the availability of household data is responsible for many of the important advances in labor economics during the past 25 years. Nonetheless, household data have disadvantages as well, and first among these is the problem of measurement error, which may have led to the appearance of "very great microlevel randomness in economic behavior" (Stafford 1986, p. 405). Aggregation can provide a way of washing out, through averaging, some of the errors that appear at the individual level, and when a unit of observation higher than the individual or household can be justified on behavioral grounds, subaggregate data can be quite useful.

In this section, we use two-digit industry data from the National Income and Product Accounts. Hence, the two-digit industry is our unit of observation. In addition to mitigating problems of measurement error, the NIPA data are capable of representing the entire private U.S. economy. We have assembled data on 54 of the two-digit nongovernmental industries for the years 1968 through 1982. Governments have been excluded from the sample examined because the vesting and funding of government pensions raise issues that are unique to the public sector. Likewise, railroads have been excluded because railroad workers' pensions are regulated separately from the pensions of all other workers in the economy. Farms and "Other services" — consisting of social services, membership organizations, and miscellaneous professional services — have been deleted because of inadequate data. A more detailed account of the data and the variables constructed from them follows.

Central to our work is the unpublished two-digit industry data on "other labor income" for 1968 through 1982, which was provided to us by the Income and Wealth Division of the Bureau of Economic Analysis.

For each two-digit industry, we obtained "employer contributions to private pension and welfare funds" divided into two categories: (a) "pension and profit-sharing," and (b) the sum of "group insurance" – which includes both group health and group life insurance – and supplemental unemployment benefits. This two-way breakdown is less than ideal because pension contributions are lumped with profit-sharing, and because life insurance and supplemental unemployment are lumped with health insurance. (That is, the Bureau of Economic Analysis does not separate health insurance from life insurance and supplemental unemployment at the two-digit industry level.) Nonetheless, the breakdown improves on that used in previous research, and the problems of having health contributions lumped with life insurance and supplemental unemployment benefits are minimized by the dominance of health contributions within that category. (For example, in 1982, health contributions were 89.6 percent of the sum of health, life, and supplemental unemployment benefits in the aggregate economy.)[3]

From these unpublished data and the published NIPA data, the following variables needed to estimate the model stated as equations (2.34) and (2.35) can be constructed for each two-digit industry in each year.

1. *Relative Prices.* Recall from equations (2.5) and (2.36) that four variables (c_w, c_r, c_h, and t) are required to construct the relative prices (p_r/p_w) and (p_h/p_w). We will assume, as already discussed, that (c_r/c_w) equals one, which means we need only estimates of c_h and t.

The employer's cost of providing health benefits (c_h) can be measured both over time and from industry to industry at a point in time. Variation over time is measured by observing the price index for health insurance published in the NIPA (U.S. Department of Commerce, Bureau of Economic Analysis, 1986, Table 7.10). Variation in the cost of health insurance from industry to industry is measured by using the hedonic model of health insurance cost, described in the appendix to this chapter. Readers of the appendix will see that interindustry differences in the cost of health insurance are derived only for 1977–78. Consequently, it is necessary to assume that these interindustry differences are constant over all years from 1968 through 1982.[4] These constant interindustry differences are adjusted upward or downward for each year by the health insurance price index in the NIPA. Hence, the cost of health insurance matched to each industry in each year depends on both the industry and the year of the observation.

The marginal tax rate on earnings (t) is computed under two alternative tax schemes, in an effort to test the sensitivity of the results to different assumptions about the tax filing status of the average worker in each industry.[5] The idea is to obtain an upper and lower bound on the marginal tax rate faced by the average worker in each industry. Under the *joint-filing tax scheme*, it is assumed that the average worker filed a joint return with three exemptions, and took the minimum standard deduction, low-income allowance, or zero-bracket amount (whichever was most favorable). Accordingly, taxable income, computed as yearly gross earnings minus exemptions and deductions, is applied to the tax table for a married individual filing a joint return. Under the *separate-filing tax scheme*, it is assumed that the average worker was married filing separately, took two exemptions, and again took the minimum standard deduction, low-income allowance, or zero-bracket amount. In this latter case, the computed taxable income figure is applied to the tax table for a married individual filing a separate return. Under both tax schemes, tax credits in effect during 1975 through 1978 are accounted for, as are the tax surcharges of 1968 and 1969, but no attempt is made to account for the Earned Income Tax Credit in effect in 1975 and following years.

We have *not* added the social security payroll tax rate to the marginal tax rate on wages when earnings are below the social security maximum earnings base. This amounts to assuming that workers receive an actuarially fair return on their social security contributions. Burkhauser and Turner (1985), Gordon (1983), and Sloan and Adamache (1986) have favored this assumption, based on the logic that the social security benefit formula links a worker's social security benefits to payroll taxes paid. Indeed, most current retirees are receiving more than an actuarially fair return on their social security payroll taxes; it is only for workers born after 1945 that social security will provide a return that is actuarially unfair.

Two alternatives to assuming that workers receive an actuarially fair return to social security have been developed and tested by Hamermesh and Woodbury (1990). One alternative is to add the social security payroll tax rate to the marginal tax rate paid on earned income whenever a worker's earnings fall below the social security maximum earnings base. (That is, t in equations (2.5) and (2.36) would include the payroll tax.) Two assumptions underlie this alternative: that the social security payroll tax does not apply to benefits, hence adding to the incentive to receive benefits; and that workers receive an actuarially fair return on their share (50 percent) of the payroll tax. The other alternative, first used by Turner (1987), takes the further step of adding the social security payroll tax to the employer's cost of providing wages, in addition to adding the payroll tax to the marginal tax on earned income. (That is, the payroll tax is added to c_w in equations (2.5) and (2.36), in addition to being included in t.) This alternative assumes that workers bear the full burden of the tax but will never receive any benefits, and reflects the way most college students seem to perceive the social security system.

As it turns out, estimates of the demand for fringe benefits are remarkably insensitive to these alternative ways of handling the social security payroll tax. For example, Hamermesh and Woodbury (1990) find that estimates of the uncompensated price elasticities using the three alternatives are within 3 percent of each other. Similarly, Woodbury and Bettinger (1991) find that estimated responses of fringe benefit coverage to the tax-price of benefits are virtually identical under the three alternatives. Accordingly, even though we have not performed sensitivity tests on the estimates reported in this chapter, we feel reasonably confident that our results would be unchanged if we handled the social security payroll tax differently.

2. *Compensation Shares.* The share of compensation received as pension benefits by the average worker in each industry (s_r) is obtained by dividing pension contributions per employee by total compensation per employee.[6] Total compensation per employee is defined as the sum of after-tax wages and salaries per employee, pension contributions per

employee, and insurance contributions per employee. After-tax wages and salaries are not observed directly, but are imputed in the process of assigning the marginal tax rate to the average worker in each industry (see the discussion of Relative Prices above). Similarly, the share of compensation received as health benefits (s_h) is constructed by dividing insurance contributions per employee by total compensation per employee. These shares are the dependent variables in equations (2.34) and (2.35).

3. *Real Total Compensation*. The measure of real total compensation (m/P^*) is obtained by summing after-tax earnings with employer contributions to pension and health insurance plans, and dividing by the approximated price index P^*. Note that m is the same as the denominator of the compensation shares, s_r and s_h. Because our data span 1969 through 1982, it is necessary to adjust P^* by the Consumer Price Index (CPI). Specifically, in equation (2.20), p_w and p_r are both multiplied by the CPI (divided by 100) for the appropriate year. Since p_h already incorporates the health insurance component of the CPI, no further adjustment to p_h is required.

4. *Control Variables*. The above variables, which are essential to the model and are derived from the NIPA, are supplemented by additional control variables. These variables, which are the x_ks in equations (2.34) and (2.35), are described presently. The source of each, if other than the NIPA, is noted.

First, a set of dummy variables, one for each two-digit industry in the sample, is included to control for features of an industry that do not change over time and that are either unmeasurable or difficult to measure. Inclusion of these variables yields a so-called fixed-effects model (see, for example, Johnston 1984, pp. 396–407, for a lucid exposition). It should be noted that these industry dummies are the only control variables that do not vary over time. The remaining x_ks will hence be referred to as time-varying control variables.

Second, the proportion of workers in each industry who are blue-collar workers, and the proportion of workers in each industry who are women, are both derived from *Employment and Earnings* (U.S. Department of Labor, Bureau of Labor Statistics, various March issues). These variables offer a way of controlling for characteristics of each industry's workforce that do vary over time, particularly over the business cycle, and that may influence the shares of compensation received in various forms.[7]

Third, for each industry and each year, the median ages of men and of women are approximated by taking published data from the 1970 and 1980 decennial Censuses of Population on the median age of men and women by industry, and forming a trend. From this trend, one can interpolate to obtain values for years between 1970 and 1980, and extrapolate (using the trend that prevailed between 1970 and 1980) to obtain values for years earlier than 1970 and later than 1980.[8] (The data come from U.S. Department of Commerce, Bureau of the Census 1972, 1982.)

Fourth, the average number of workers per establishment is computed for each industry in each year by taking annual data on the number of employees and number of establishments in each industry from *County Business Patterns* (U.S. Department of Commerce, Bureau of the Census, various years). This allows us to control for and appraise the existence of scale economies in the provision of benefits, which were first studied systematically by Mitchell and Andrews (1981).

Fifth, the business cycle may affect the degree to which pension liabilities are funded, or the degree to which health insurance benefits are provided or enhanced. In order to account for variation over the cycle in fringe benefit provision, we include as a control variable the annual proportional change in real Gross National Product contributed by the industry. (Note that, as a result, observations from 1968 are dropped from the sample, leaving us with a sample of observations from 1969 through 1982.) Also, in order to account for any exogenous trends in fringe benefits, a simple time trend is included among the x_ks.

Finally, we attempt to control for the level of firm-specific human capital possessed by the average worker in each industry. This is important because Lazear (1981), among others, has hypothesized that the greater the amount of firm-specific human capital possessed by a worker, the greater will be the incentive for the worker's employer to offer compensation in a deferred form such as pensions. The reasoning is that deferred compensation creates an incentive to workers who possess large stocks of specific human capital to remain with the firm (see Allen and Clark 1987 for a review). This line of reasoning is known as the "agency hypothesis."

Given the popularity of the agency hypothesis as an explanation of why firms offer deferred compensation, it is interesting that it has rarely been tested (but see Mumy and Manson 1985). Part of the reason for the rarity of testing the agency hypothesis is that finding good proxies for firm-specific human capital is no easy matter. Parsons (1972), in his pioneering effort to test for the effects of specific capital, focused on capital per worker, job tenure, and occupational category (for example, the proportion of managers in an industry) as variables likely to be more highly correlated with specific than with general human capital. Long and Scott (1982, p. 215), in their work on tax incentives for provision of fringe benefits, approximated firm-specific human capital with a capital-labor ratio constructed by dividing real corporate capital consumption allowance (in $1,000,000s) by the number of full-time equivalent employees (both obtained from the NIPA). We follow their practice, except, of course, the measure of capital consumption allowance per worker used here is disaggregated by industry, rather than for the economy as a whole.[9] Also, we recognize that the capital-labor ratio is an imperfect proxy for firm-specific human capital, and that it is open to alternative interpretations.[10]

Descriptive statistics for each variable used in the analysis are displayed in table 3.1. Except as noted in the table notes, the means displayed are weighted by the number of employees in each industry.[11]

Results from the National Income and Product Accounts

The results of estimating the demand system specified by equations (2.34) and (2.35) are displayed in table 3.2. Note that four sets of estimates are shown. The first two columns (labeled "Joint-Filing Tax Scheme") are estimated with marginal taxes on wage income (and the

Table 3.1 Descriptive Statistics of Variables in the NIPA Data

Variable	Mean	Standard Deviation	Minimum	Maximum
Variables from joint tax scheme:				
s_w (wage share)	0.903	0.055	0.627	0.980
s_r (pension share)	0.050	0.037	0.002	0.311
s_h (health insurance share)	0.047	0.025	0.001	0.140
p_r/p_w	0.797	0.029	0.610	0.850
p_h/p_w	0.811	0.101	0.570	1.138
m/P^* (real total compensation, $)	14,815	3,641	7,869	31,938
Variables from separate tax scheme:				
s_w (wage share)	0.895	0.060	0.589	0.979
s_r (pension share)	0.054	0.040	0.002	0.338
s_h (health insurance share)	0.050	0.028	0.001	0.158
p_r/p_w	0.693	0.072	0.460	0.810
p_h/p_w	0.706	0.121	0.416	1.066
m/P^* (real total compensation, $)	12,054	2,547	7,371	24,592
Variables common to both tax schemes:				
Proportion of workers blue-collar	0.677	0.280	0.0	0.930
Proportion of workers female	0.344	0.215	0.0	0.846
Age of male workers (industry median)	37.10	2.97	29.60	49.80
Age of female workers (industry median)	35.68	2.84	26.20	47.10
Average number workers per establishment	16.26	20.08	3.30	323.15
Capital-labor ratio	5,549	12,551	0.00	112,679
Annual proportional change in industry output	0.023	0.071	−0.395	0.340

NOTES: All means are weighted by the number of employees in each industry, except for average number of workers per establishment (which is weighted by the number of firms in the industry), the capital-labor ratio, and the annual proportional change in industry output (both of which are unweighted). There are 54 industries in the sample, with observations from 1969 through 1982 (inclusive). Hence $N=756$.

derived tax-price of wage income) constructed by applying taxable income to the married joint-filing tax schedule. The second two columns (labeled "Separate-Filing Tax Scheme") are estimated using marginal taxes constructed by applying taxable income to the married separate-filing tax schedule. The first and second columns differ in that the first column displays estimates obtained by applying Zellner's joint generalized least squares estimator to the data (labeled "JGLS"), whereas the second column displays *weighted* joint generalized least squares estimates (labeled "WJGLS"). The same difference distinguishes the third column from the fourth. Weighted estimates were obtained out of a concern that the error terms in equations (2.34) and (2.35) might be heteroscedastic. Specifically, it stands to reason that the variance of the error term might be larger in small industries than in large industries. The solution is to implement weighted least squares, with industry total compensation serving as the weight. The results suggest that at most a minor gain in efficiency is obtained from the correction for heteroscedasticity.

1. *Relations Between Control Variables and Fringe Benefit Shares*. It is useful to examine first the coefficients of the additional time-varying explanatory variables; that is, the x_ks. Coefficients of the time-varying control variables appear under the headings "Variables in the Pension Equation" and "Variables in the Health Insurance Equation" of table 3.2. (Coefficients of the industry dummy variables are excluded from table 3.2 to conserve space, and will not be discussed.)

A higher proportion of blue-collar workers in an industry appears to be related to a higher proportion of compensation received as pension benefits, but to a lower proportion of compensation received as health benefits. Thus, blue-collar workers appear to be favored relative to white-collar workers in the provision of pension benefits, whereas white-collar workers appear to be favored relative to blue-collar workers in the provision of health insurance benefits, other things equal. Because these results differ both from the findings of earlier studies and from findings presented below (using the 1977 EEEC), it seems best to

Table 3.2 Estimates Coefficients of the Fringe Benefit Demand System Applied to NIPA Data

Parameter or Variable	Joint-Filing Tax Scheme		Separate-Filing Tax Scheme	
	JGLS	WJGLS	JGLS	WJGLS
a_w	2.3303	2.1382	2.5210	2.2853
	(0.0555)	(0.0479)	(0.0563)	(0.0485)
a_r	-0.9315	-0.6845	-1.1066	-0.8463
	(0.0616)	(0.0484)	(0.0644)	(0.0511)
a_h	-0.3988	-0.4537	-0.4144	-0.4390
	(0.0542)	(0.0509)	(0.0553)	(0.0505)
b_{ww}	-0.0751	-0.1052	-0.1351	-0.1248
	(0.0127)	(0.0107)	(0.0074)	(0.0063)
b_{wr}	0.0665	0.1046	0.1253	0.1218
	(0.0129)	(0.0150)	(0.0077)	(0.0065)
b_{wh}	0.0086	0.0006	0.0098	0.0030
	(0.0032)	(0.0026)	(0.0032)	(0.0026)
b_{rr}	-0.0506	-0.0947	-0.1082	-0.1108
	(0.0138)	(0.0115)	(0.0092)	(0.0075)
b_{rh}	-0.0159	-0.0099	-0.0171	-0.0110
	(0.0037)	(0.0026)	(0.0039)	(0.0029)
b_{hh}	0.0073	0.0093	0.0073	0.0080
	(0.0033)	(0.0028)	(0.0036)	(0.0030)
b_w	-0.1281	-0.1119	-0.1463	-0.1246
	(0.0058)	(0.0052)	(0.0058)	(0.0052)
b_r	0.0906	0.0715	0.1081	0.0893
	(0.0064)	(0.0052)	(0.0067)	(0.0055)
b_h	0.0375	0.0404	0.0382	0.0353
	(0.0056)	(0.0055)	(0.0057)	(0.0052)
Variables in the Pension Equation:				
Proportion of workers	0.0052	0.0054	0.0067	0.0051
blue-collar	(0.0022)	(0.0016)	(0.0023)	(0.0017)
Proportion of workers female	0.0030	-0.0061	0.0061	-0.0016
	(0.0077)	(0.0066)	(0.0081)	(0.0072)
Age of male workers	0.0014	0.0005	0.0015	0.0005
	(0.0004)	(0.0003)	(0.0004)	(0.0004)
Age of female workers	0.0008	-0.0002	0.0008	-0.0003
	(0.0003)	(0.0003)	(0.0003)	(0.0003)
Average number workers	-0.0421	-0.1460	-0.0466	-0.1470
per establishment (1,000s)	(0.0315)	(0.0291)	(0.0336)	(0.0320)
Capital-labor ratio	1.6600	1.2700	1.6600	1.2800
(1,000,000s)	(0.1130)	(0.1510)	(0.1240)	(0.1670)

Table 3.2 (continued)

Parameter or Variable	Joint-Filing Tax Scheme		Separate-Filing Tax Scheme	
	JGLS	WJGLS	JGLS	WJGLS
Annual proportional change	0.0024	0.0065	0.0053	0.0093
in industry output	(0.0049)	(0.0038)	(0.0052)	(0.0041)
Time trend	0.0010	0.0008	0.0011	0.0008
	(0.0002)	(0.0001)	(0.0002)	(0.0002)
Variables in the Health Insurance Equation:				
Proportion of workers	−0.0130	−0.0099	−0.0148	−0.0111
blue-collar	(0.0019)	(0.0016)	(0.0021)	(0.0018)
Proportion of workers female	0.0171	0.0169	0.0129	0.0127
	(0.0068)	(0.0071)	(0.0072)	(0.0077)
Age of male workers	0.0027	0.0022	0.0027	0.0025
	(0.0003)	(0.0004)	(0.0004)	(0.0004)
Age of female workers	−0.0016	−0.0004	−0.0015	0.0000
	(0.0003)	(0.0003)	(0.0003)	(0.0003)
Average number workers	0.0176	0.0268	0.0132	0.0207
per establishment (1,000s)	(0.0280)	(0.0312)	(0.0303)	(0.0345)
Capital-labor ratio	−0.0655	−0.1860	−0.1080	−0.1640
	(0.1010)	(0.1610)	(0.1110)	(0.1770)
Annual proportional change	−0.0223	−0.0285	−0.0230	−0.0285
in industry output	(0.0044)	(0.0041)	(0.0047)	(0.0044)
Time trend	0.0020	0.0020	0.0029	0.0032
	(0.0001)	(0.0001)	(0.0002)	(0.0002)
Mean squared error:				
Pension equation	0.00008	0.5197	0.00009	0.6215
Health equation	0.00006	0.5982	0.00007	0.7255
R-squared:				
Pension equation	0.9617	0.9752	0.9629	0.9752
Health equation	0.9090	0.9394	0.9107	0.9393

NOTES: Estimates result from applying an iterative version of Zellner's seemingly unrelated regression procedure to equations (2.34) and (2.35). "Joint-Filing Tax Scheme" indicates that marginal tax rates (and the implied tax-price of wages) are obtained by applying taxable income to the married joint-filing tax schedule; "Separate-Filing Tax Scheme" indicates that the married separate-filing schedule is used. JGLS denotes unweighted joint generalized least squares estimates, and WJGLS denotes joint generalized least squares estimates weighted by total compensation. The dependent variables are shares of total compensation received as pensions and as health insurance. Asymptotic standard error of each coefficient is shown in parentheses.

Coefficients of the nonprice variables (shown under "Variables in the Pension Equation" and "Variables in the Health Equation") are interpretable simply as the change in the share of total compensation received as pension benefits (or as health insurance benefits) resulting from a unit change in the independent variable, all else equal.

Each equation includes a set of two-digit industry dummy variables, in addition to the time-varying control variables shown.

defer discussion of the occupational effects to the Comparative Discussion section.

A higher proportion of female workers in an industry may increase the share of compensation received as health insurance, but appears to bear little relation to the share of compensation received as pensions. The former finding conflicts with the notion that women often rely on the health insurance of their spouses. The simplest interpretation of the finding is that health insurance benefits are often a fixed sum that varies little from worker to worker within an establishment. Health insurance benefits, provided as such a fixed sum, would be a greater proportion of the relatively low total compensation received by women. This interpretation is further discussed later in the chapter.

An aging male workforce may increase very slightly the share of compensation received as pensions, and appears to increase the share of health insurance benefits by .2 or .3 percentage point. The median age of women in an industry appears to be quite weakly related to the share of compensation received as either pension or health insurance benefits, although there is some evidence that an aging female workforce may slightly decrease the share of compensation received as health insurance. This last is an entirely plausible finding, in that women have traditionally incurred relatively large health care costs during the child-bearing years.

The findings on establishment size reported in table 3.2 are strikingly at odds with earlier work on fringe benefit determination. First, industries whose establishments are on average larger appear to pay a *lower* proportion of compensation in the form of pension benefits. And second, there is no statistically significant relationship between establishment size and health insurance benefits. (The point estimates do suggest that an increase in establishment size of 1,000 workers may tend to increase the share of total compensation received as health insurance benefits by 1 percentage point, but the standard errors of the estimates are large.) These surprising establishment size relationships are discussed further below.

The estimated relations between the capital-labor ratio and fringe benefit shares are striking. The results consistently indicate that a higher capital-labor ratio leads to a greater proportion of total compensation paid as pensions – that is, as deferred benefits. In contrast, a higher capital-labor ratio appears to have no consistent relationship with the share of compensation paid as health benefits – that is, as current benefits. If the measure of the capital-labor ratio is properly interpreted as representing the level of firm-specific human capital in an industry, then the results are consistent with the presence of a strong agency incentive to offer deferred benefits.

The annual proportional change in industry output is positively related to the pension share of total compensation, but negatively related to the health benefit share. Together, these results suggest that firms tend to fund pension liabilities when it is most convenient to do so – that is, when business is good – but that health benefits are treated as a fixed cost that is paid regardless of business conditions.[12]

Finally, the time trend variable shows that there has been a positive secular trend in the provision of both pensions and health insurance. For both pensions and health insurance, the annual increase is small – only .1 or .2 percentage point per year – but statistically significantly different from zero. Moreover, it is worth bearing in mind that .1 percentage point per year accumulates rapidly over time into important increases in the share of compensation received as fringe benefits.

2. *Price, Income, and Substitution Elasticities.* The effects of taxes and income on the shares of compensation received as pensions and health insurance are best seen by transforming the parameters shown in table 3.2 into appropriate elasticities. Compensated price elasticities (η_{ij}^*), uncompensated price elasticities (η_{ij}), income elasticities (η_{im}), and elasticities of substitution (σ_{ij}), all computed at the sample mean, are displayed in table 3.3, and the standard error of each elasticity is shown in parentheses below each elasticity. (See chapter 2 for a discussion of how these standard errors were computed.) The elasticities displayed in the four columns of table 3.3 correspond to the parameter estimates given in the four columns of table 3.2.

Although the compensated and uncompensated price elasticities $(\eta_{ij}^*,$ and $\eta_{ij})$ are of intrinsic interest, they can be derived by the Slutsky

Table 3.3 Price, Income, and Substitution Elasticities
Computed from Fringe Benefit Demand System
Applied to NIPA Data

	Joint-Filing Tax Scheme		Separate-Filing Tax Scheme	
	JGLS	WJGLS	JGLS	WJGLS
Compensated Price Elasticities:				
η_{ww}^*	−0.17	−0.21	−0.25	−0.24
	(0.07)	(0.07)	(0.08)	(0.07)
η_{rr}^*	−1.95	−2.84	−2.94	−2.99
	(0.94)	(1.68)	(1.77)	(1.81)
η_{hh}^*	−0.80	−0.75	−0.80	−0.79
	(0.10)	(0.10)	(0.09)	(0.08)
η_{wr}^*	0.12	0.16	0.20	0.19
	(0.05)	(0.05)	(0.06)	(0.06)
η_{rw}^*	2.21	2.99	3.20	3.14
	(1.21)	(1.87)	(2.06)	(2.00)
η_{wh}^*	0.06	0.05	0.06	0.05
	(0.03)	(0.03)	(0.03)	(0.03)
η_{hw}^*	1.09	0.92	1.10	0.95
	(0.17)	(0.08)	(0.18)	(0.10)
η_{rh}^*	−0.27	−0.15	−0.26	−0.16
	(0.29)	(0.19)	(0.29)	(0.20)
η_{hr}^*	−0.30	−0.17	−0.29	−0.17
	(0.23)	(0.15)	(0.23)	(0.16)
Uncompensated Price Elasticities:				
η_{ww}	−0.95	−1.00	−1.00	−1.01
	(0.01)	(0.01)	(0.01)	(0.01)
η_{rr}	−2.09	−2.96	−3.10	−3.13
	(0.90)	(1.64)	(1.73)	(1.77)
η_{hh}	−0.88	−0.84	−0.89	−0.88
	(0.11)	(0.12)	(0.11)	(0.10)
η_{wr}	0.08	0.12	0.15	0.14
	(0.02)	(0.02)	(0.02)	(0.02)
η_{rw}	−0.31	0.80	0.52	0.77
	(0.45)	(0.68)	(0.37)	(0.58)
η_{wh}	0.02	0.01	0.02	0.01
	(0.01)	(0.004)	(0.01)	(0.01)
η_{hw}	−0.55	−0.77	−0.50	−0.57
	(0.36)	(0.46)	(0.33)	(0.35)

Table 3.3 (*continued*)

	Joint-Filing Tax Scheme		Separate-Filing Tax Scheme	
	JGLS	WJGLS	JGLS	WJGLS
η_{rh}	-0.40	-0.26	-0.41	-0.29
	(0.33)	(0.22)	(0.34)	(0.24)
η_{hr}	-0.39	-0.26	-0.39	-0.26
	(0.21)	(0.14)	(0.22)	(0.14)
Income Elasticities:				
η_{wm}	0.86	0.88	0.84	0.86
	(0.01)	(0.01)	(0.01)	(0.01)
η_{rm}	2.79	2.43	2.99	2.65
	(1.54)	(1.23)	(1.72)	(1.42)
η_{hm}	1.82	1.87	1.78	1.70
	(0.46)	(0.48)	(0.45)	(0.39)
Elasticities of Substitution:				
σ_{wr}	2.46	3.31	3.58	3.51
	(1.19)	(1.88)	(2.06)	(2.00)
σ_{wh}	1.21	1.02	1.22	1.07
	(0.13)	(0.06)	(0.13)	(0.07)
σ_{rh}	-5.85	-3.24	-5.43	-3.01
	(8.39)	(5.20)	(7.97)	(4.96)
Sample Mean Shares:				
s_w	0.9037	0.9031	0.8966	0.8953
s_r	0.0505	0.0502	0.0542	0.0543
s_h	0.0458	0.0467	0.0491	0.0505

NOTES: Elasticities computed from the parameter estimated displayed in table 3.2. (See chapter 2 for a discussion of the elasticities and details of their computation.) Standard error of each elasticity is in parentheses below each elasticity. (Standard errors are computed by taking a Taylor approximation at the sample mean.)

equation from the compensation shares, the income elasticities (η_{im}), and the elasticities of substitution (σ_{ij}). As a result, it is useful to focus on the latter two elasticities.

The estimated income elasticities of demand for wages, pensions, and health insurance are similar in each of the four estimated equation systems. There is strong evidence that the demand for wage benefits is income inelastic, with a point estimate of η_{wm} around 0.85. The demands for pensions and for health insurance, on the other hand, appear to be income elastic. Looking at the point estimates, the results suggest that the demand for pensions is highly income elastic, with estimates of η_{rm} in the range of 2.5 to 3.0. The demand for health insurance is also income elastic, although the point estimates of η_{hm} are lower—in the range of 1.7 to 1.9. Note that the income elasticities of demand for pensions are statistically significantly different from *unity* at no better than the 12-percent level using a two-tailed test, whereas the income elasticities of demand for health insurance are statistically significantly different from *unity* at better than the 10-percent level (again using a two-tailed test). Hence, although the point estimates of the income elasticity of demand for health insurance are smaller, they are statistically somewhat stronger.

The high estimated income elasticities of demand for pensions and health insurance—and the correspondingly low income elasticity of demand for wage income—are striking because they suggest that the growth of pensions during the post-World War II era cannot be explained by rising marginal income tax rates alone. On the contrary, the income elasticities imply that a 100 percent increase in total compensation would lead to a near doubling of health insurance benefits, and possibly as much as a tripling of pension benefits. The same 100 percent increase in total compensation would result in only an 85 percent increase in wage benefits. Although these findings accord with some earlier income elasticity estimates (Woodbury 1983), the findings conflict with certain others (Long and Scott 1982).

The estimated elasticities of substitution (σ_{ij}) suggest a rather simple and intuitively appealing structure of workers' preferences for wages, pensions, and health insurance. Pensions and health insurance benefits may be weakly complementary, as indicated by the negative estimated σ_{rh}s. Note that although these point estimates are negative, they have high standard errors, and are not statistically significantly different from zero. Pensions and health insurance benefits both substitute for wages, and the point estimates suggest that pensions and wages may be better substitutes than health benefits and wages. Although the standard errors of both σ_{wr} and σ_{wh} suggest strongly that both substitution elasticities exceed *zero*, the evidence that σ_{wr} and σ_{wh} exceed *unity* is less strong. Thus, although we can conclude with some confidence that both pensions and health insurance are substitutes for wages, we must be more tentative in concluding that the possibilities for substitution between wages and either form of fringe benefit are great.

There are no existing estimates with which these substitution elasticities can be compared. But they do tell a logical and intuitively appealing story. Any change that leads to greater pension benefits leads also to more health insurance (and conversely). In that retirement income is more likely to be enjoyed if one has good health care, and since good health care leads to the expectation of a longer retirement, this result makes good sense. Likewise, it makes sense that wages and pensions should be better substitutes than wages and health benefits. Health benefits, in that they are benefits in-kind, are restrictive and specific. Pensions, on the other hand, are properly thought of as cash income with one restriction—that the income be spent in retirement.

Estimates from the Survey of
Employer Expenditures for Employee Compensation

Description of the Data

The Survey of Employer Expenditures for Employee Compensation (EEEC) was a survey of establishments conducted by the Bureau of Labor Statistics from 1966 through 1977. The 1977 EEEC sampled 3,320 establishments of all sizes in order to obtain detailed data on wages and fringe benefits.[13] The main advantage of the EEEC is that it includes data on dollar expenditures on fringe benefits, as opposed to merely whether fringe benefits were provided. Hence, it allows one to observe the shares of compensation received as pensions, health insurance, and so on.

The main shortcoming of the EEEC is that it contains no data on the characteristics of the employees of each establishment. But it does include industry, region, occupation, and urban-nonurban location identifiers that permit one to match each record with average employee characteristics obtained from a separate source. In order to partially remedy the deficiencies of the EEEC for research, several researchers – including Alpert (1983), Antos (1981), Freeman (1981), and Sloan and Adamache (1986) – have successfully matched the EEEC data with various group means tabulated from the Current Population Survey.

This section presents estimates of fringe benefit demand derived from a sample of 5,234 *groups of workers* from the 1977 EEEC. It is important to understand that although the EEEC are establishment-level data, we actually observe workers disaggregated into two groups in each establishment – blue-collar workers and white-collar workers.[14] Hence, the unit of observation is not the establishment per se, but either a group of blue-collar workers, or a group of white-collar workers, observed in an establishment surveyed in the EEEC.

Each EEEC worker-group record is supplemented with data from the 1977 Current Population Survey and the 1977–78 National Medical Care Expenditure Survey. Specifically, appropriate group means of certain variables tabulated from the Current Population Survey are matched to each EEEC worker-group record. The match between the EEEC worker-group and the Current Population Survey was carried out as follows. From the Current Population Survey, means of the required variables were computed for 848 groups of workers. The 848 groups result from dividing all workers in the Current Population Survey into 53 two-digit industries of employment, 4 regions of residence (northeast, north central, south, and west), 2 occupations (white-collar or blue-collar), and 2 locations (either within or outside of a Standard Metropolitan Statistical Area). The mean for each group of workers was then matched with the appropriate EEEC worker-group. For example, the mean years of schooling of urban blue-collar workers in printing and publishing in the north central states was matched with all EEEC worker-group observations that were of urban blue-collar workers in printing and publishing in the north central states. Also, the appropriate value of the hedonic price index of health insurance, created from the from the National Medical Care Expenditure Survey was matched with each EEEC record. (See the appendix to this chapter for details.)

This procedure of matching group means from a secondary data set with micro data (that is, either individual or establishment data) has been referred to as "data-stretching" by Greenberg, Pollard, and Alpert (1989). Their investigation of the statistical problems that arise from data-stretching suggests that the coefficients of stretched variables may be biased, and that the standard errors of the coefficients of stretched variables are biased downward. (Moulton 1990 has reached a similar conclusion regarding the standard errors of the coefficients of stretched variables.) Greenberg, Pollard, and Alpert conclude that data-stretching is a procedure whose routine use should be avoided, although they defend the practice as a means of reducing the variance of estimates. Clearly, data-stretching is not a practice that anyone would undertake if adequate data were available. We defend our use of stretching in this context because it allows us to include controls—albeit imperfect—for schooling, gender, race, and age that would otherwise be excluded. Greenberg, Pollard, and Alpert's results make us especially cautious in drawing inferences from these stretched variables.

Since 3,320 establishments were surveyed in the 1977 EEEC, as many as 6,640 groups of workers could have been analyzed—a group of blue-collar workers and a group of white-collar workers in each establishment. However, for three reasons the final sample includes only 5,234 worker-groups. First, not all establishments employed both types of workers; such establishments contribute only one observation to the sample. Second, not all EEEC worker-group records included all the industry, region, and location data needed to make a match with the means tabulated from the Current Population Survey or with the appropriate value of the hedonic price index. Third, in order to make the sample similar to the NIPA sample in its industrial composition, worker-groups in railroads, certain service industries (education; religious, welfare, and membership organizations; and miscellaneous professional services), and government were deleted from the sample.

The following variables needed to estimate the fringe benefit demand model (eq. 2.34 and eq. 2.35) can be constructed using the data base obtained by matching and merging the 1977 EEEC, the 1977 Current Population Survey, and the 1977–78 National Medical Care Expenditure Survey.

1. *Relative Prices.* Recall again that four variables (c_w, c_r, c_h, and t) are required to construct the relative prices (p_r/p_w) and (p_h/p_w). In using the NIPA data, we assumed that (c_r/c_w) equals one, and the same assumption will be made in using the EEEC survey. Hence, we again need estimates only of c_h and t.

Variation in the cost of health insurance (c_h) from industry to industry is measured by using the hedonic model of health insurance cost described in detail in the appendix to this chapter. The price of health insurance matched to each worker-group is based on its industry, region (northeast, north central, south, or west), location (urban or nonurban), and occupation (white-collar or blue-collar).

The marginal tax rate on earnings (t) that faces the average worker in each group in the EEEC cannot be observed directly. Hence, the marginal tax rate is computed in two quite different ways, in an effort to test the sensitivity of the results to different assumptions about the marginal tax rate facing the average worker in each group.

The first approach is to impute the marginal tax rate facing each worker-group by a rather complicated algorithm. This algorithm proceeds by first assigning certain household variables from the 1977 Current Population Survey to each EEEC worker-group. The following household variables turn out to be relevant to tax computation: (a) the mean ratio of total household income to worker's earnings; (b) the mean number of persons in the household, rounded to the nearest whole number; (c) a dummy variable equal to one if the majority of workers in the group owned their home; and (d) variables indicating the most common household arrangement of workers in the group (married with spouse present, single, or single head of household). Each of these variables is computed for each of the 848 Current Population Survey groups, and the appropriate value of each variable assigned to each EEEC worker-group.

Next, average earnings of each EEEC worker-group are multiplied by the mean ratio of total household income to worker's earnings, in order to obtain a measure of average total household income for each EEEC group. This is the basic measure of gross income from which taxes and the marginal tax rate are computed. Exemptions and deductions are computed based on the average number of persons in households in the worker-group. Either the minimum standard deduction or the average amount of itemized deductions is taken, depending on which is more advantageous and whether the average worker in the group owned his or her home. [The average deductions declared by each adjusted gross income class for interest, taxes, medical and dental expenses, and miscellaneous items are summed and applied to each worker-group by gross income class. These itemized deduction amounts for each adjusted gross income class are obtained from *Statistics of Income* (U.S. Department of the Treasury 1979).] The per capita credit in effect in 1977 and the Earned Income Tax Credit, if applicable, are computed for each worker-group (Pechman 1977, pp. 76 and 102). Taxable income is computed by subtracting exemptions, deductions, and the exemption equivalent of applicable credits from gross income. The taxable income figure is then applied to the income tax schedule for single persons, single heads of households, or married couples filing a joint return, depending on the most common household arrangement of workers in the group. The result is a marginal income tax rate (t) and a federal income tax bill for each worker-group in the EEEC sample.

The second approach to computing the marginal tax rate is somewhat simpler. As in the first approach, this approach starts by assigning to each EEEC worker-group some household information from the Current Population Survey — in this case, the mean ratio of total household income to worker's earnings is the only variable required. Average gross household income for each EEEC group is again imputed by multiplying the average earnings of each EEEC worker-group by the mean ratio of total household income to worker's earnings from the Current Population Survey. Hereafter, the second approach differs from the first. Now, the marginal tax rate (t) and the taxbill are assigned directly to each worker-group based on its imputed gross household income. The appropriate marginal tax rate and taxbill are taken from *Statistics of Income* (U.S. Department of the Treasury 1979).

To summarize, two different methods of computing the marginal tax rate (t) facing each worker-group are used in the EEEC estimation. The first relies on a fairly complicated algorithm that imputes the marginal tax rate facing each worker-group based on the existing tax code. This first approach results in what will be referred to as *imputed marginal tax rates* in what follows. The second approach assigns marginal tax rates from *Statistics of Income* directly to each worker-group based on its imputed gross household income. This second approach results in what will be referred to as *direct marginal tax rates*, since they are assigned directly from observed tax returns rather than being imputed from the tax code.

2. *Compensation Shares.* There are two different concepts of compensation share that may be relevant with the EEEC data. The first is the proportion of *each worker's* total compensation received as wages, pensions, and health insurance. The second is the proportion of *each household's* total compensation received as wages, pensions, and health insurance. The first would be relevant if we believed that choices about fringe benefits were made by individual workers independent of their household situation. The second would be relevant if we believed that choices about fringes are really household decisions. There can be little doubt that fringe benefit choices are household choices, but available data are inadequate to treat these choices in a true household framework. Rather, lack of adequate household data has forced researchers to treat fringe benefit choices as choices made by individual workers.

A compromise is, however, possible. The share of each worker-group's total compensation received as wages, pensions, and health insurance could be computed as a proportion of household total compensation, where household total compensation is defined as the income (excluding fringe benefits) of all household members plus the average fringe benefits of the worker-group. Such shares fail to consider the fringe benefits received by members of the household other than the worker in question, but may nevertheless serve two purposes. First, they may give an improved approximation to household fringe benefit shares. And second, they will certainly yield information about the sensitivity of parameter estimates to the specification of the dependent variable.

This discussion suggests that two different sets of compensation shares could be constructed and used with the EEEC survey data. The first would use the average disposable earnings of each worker-group in computing total compensation shares. For example, the share of total compensation received as pension contributions would be computed as:

$$s_r = z_r p_r / (z_w p_w + z_r p_r + z_h p_h) \tag{3.1}$$

where the notation is the same as that developed in chapter 2. In particular, $z_w p_w$ is the dollar amount of after-tax earnings received by the average member of the worker-group.

The second set of compensation shares would use the imputed household income of each worker-group in computing total compensation shares. In this latter case, the share of total compensation received as pension contributions would be computed as:

$$s_r = z_r p_r / (z_w p_w + z_r p_r + z_h p_h + I) \tag{3.2}$$

where I is the after-tax income, excluding fringe benefits, received by other household members. Again, shares computed in this second way do not truly measure the share of household total compensation received as pensions, because they fail to consider the fringe benefits received by other members of the household. But again, such shares may nevertheless give us an idea of how sensitive are estimates of the tradeoff between wages and fringe benefits to different specifications of the dependent variable.

It will be convenient to refer to shares computed with regard only to the earnings and benefits of each worker-group, as in equation (3.1), as *individual* measures of compensation shares. Shares computed with regard to all household income and each worker-group's benefits, as in equation (3.2), will be referred to as *household* measures of compensation shares.

Recall from the discussion of marginal tax rates in the subsection on Relative Prices that we have two methods of computing the taxes paid by each worker-group: One method uses an imputation based on the tax code, and the other method assigns an observed marginal tax rate directly to each worker-group based on its gross household income. Hence, there will be two ways of computing the *individual* compensation shares from equation (3.1), since $z_w p_w$, which is after-tax earnings, will differ depending on the method of computing taxes. Also, there will be two ways of computing the *household* compensation shares from equation (3.2), since $z_w p_w$ and I will both differ depending on the method of computing taxes.

As a result, four separate sets of compensation shares are computed in the EEEC data base, as follows: (a) individual compensation shares that use imputed tax rates to calculate after-tax earnings; (b) household compensation shares that use imputed tax rates to calculate after-tax earnings; (c) individual compensation shares that use direct tax rates to calculate after-tax earnings; and (d) household compensation shares that use direct tax rates to calculate after-tax earnings. These four sets of compensation shares will result in four different sets of estimates of equations (2.34) and (2.35).

3. Real Total Compensation. The real total compensation variable (m/P^*) poses a problem in the EEEC data because it is likely to be correlated with the error term. To see why, consider an establishment that offers its workers unusually generous pension and health insurance benefits, and think of this generosity as a positive disturbance to the random error terms u_r and u_h in equations (2.34) and (2.35). For a given level of wages, both total compensation and the shares of total compensation received as pensions and health insurance by workers in such an establishment will be high. Hence, there is simultaneity between the fringe benefit shares and total compensation: Our model implies that total compensation affects the fringe benefit shares, and now it appears that—in a stochastic setting in which compensation shares experience random disturbances—the shares may affect total compensation. Hence, total compensation is no longer independent of the error terms.

This is a significant problem when one uses establishment-level data, because such random disturbances are likely to be significant at the establishment level. With industry-level data, much of the random error is washed out in aggregation to the industry level. Hence, there was no need to consider this problem when estimating the model using the NIPA data.

The endogeneity of total compensation in the establishment-level data is handled here by the method of instrumental variables. Total compensation (m) of workers in each worker-group is constructed in the usual way by summing average after-tax earnings of workers in the group with average employer contributions to retirement, health insurance, and savings and thrift plans. (There are actually four measures of total compensation, one corresponding to each of the four sets of compensation shares discussed in the previous section.) The *instrument* for total compensation, denoted by m', is the after-tax earnings of the average worker in the worker-group divided by the two-digit *industry average share* of total compensation received as wages. The resulting variable, m', is highly correlated with actual total compensation, but uncorrelated with the error terms. Indeed, m' seems a nearly ideal instrument for m. Use of the industry average share of wages in computing total compensation purges the correlation between m' and the error terms. But m' still incorporates some establishment level information about the total compensation of each worker-group, because the numerator of m' is average after-tax wages for the worker-group.

4. *Control Variables*. The above variables are essential to the model and are derived from the EEEC survey with some supplementation from the CPS and *Statistics of Income*. These variables are further supplemented by additional control variables from the EEEC, the CPS, and the National Medical Care Expenditure Survey. Again, these control variables are the x_ks in equations (2.34) and (2.35).

First, several variables are available directly from the EEEC file, and are specific to each worker-group record. These variables are: (a) the number of employees in each establishment, which is included to control for economies of scale in the provision of fringe benefits, (b) a dummy variable equal to one if the workers in the unit were covered by a collective bargaining contract, (c) a dummy variable equal to one if the worker-group was composed of white-collar workers, (d) a dummy variable equal to one if the unit was located in a Standard Metropolitan Statistical Area (SMSA), and (e) a set of dummy variables modeling the regional location of the worker-group (northeast, north central, south, or west).

Second, Alpert (1982, pp. 186–187) has suggested that the ratio of paid leave hours (vacation, holiday, sick leave, and personal leave) to total hours worked is a good proxy for the level of firm-specific human capital possessed by a group of workers. His reasoning is that paid leave time tends to increase with job tenure, and hence should be highly correlated with job-specific skills. It is possible to compute this ratio variable for each worker-group in the EEEC sample using available data. The resulting ratio variable, which will be referred to as the "skill proxy," is included among the x_ks.

Third, because part-time workers often fail to qualify for certain fringe benefit plans, it is important to control for the presence of part-time workers in each worker-group. A variable measuring the prevalence of part-time workers in each worker-group can be constructed from the EEEC data. The variable is constructed by dividing the total number of workers in the group (both full-time and part-time) by the estimated number of full-time equivalent workers in the group. The larger the value of this variable, the greater the proportion of part-time workers in the group.

Fourth, as noted above, several group means tabulated from the 1977 Current Population Survey are matched with each EEEC worker-group record. The variables added to each EEEC record in this way are: (a) average number of years of schooling, (b) proportion of workers who are female, (c) proportion of workers who are white, (d) proportion of workers under age 30, and (e) proportion of workers over age 50. Addition of these variables is an attempt to overcome the lack of data on characteristics of workers in each group. As discussed above, coefficients of these "stretched" variables should be interpreted with caution.

Finally, a set of 50 two-digit industry dummy variables was included to control for otherwise unmeasured differences that might exist across industries. (Fifty-one two-digit industries are represented in the sample; the dummy variable for metal mining is omitted from the estimation.)

Descriptive statistics for each variable used in the analysis are displayed in table 3.4. The means displayed are all simple averages of the worker-groups in the sample.

Results from the Survey of Employer Expenditures for Employee Compensation

The results of applying the two-equation demand system specified by equations (2.34) and (2.35) to the EEEC survey data are displayed in table 3.5. Four sets of estimates are shown. The first two columns— labeled "Imputed Tax Rates"—display estimates obtained with marginal taxes on wage income and the derived tax-price of wage income imputed by the algorithm described above. The second two columns—labeled "Direct Tax Rates"—display estimates obtained with marginal taxes assigned directly from *Statistics of Income* based on gross household income. The first and second columns differ in that the first column displays estimates obtained using individual compensation shares defined by equation (3.1) as the dependent variables, whereas the second column displays estimates obtained using household compensation shares defined by equation (3.2). The same difference distinguishes the third column from the fourth. All estimates shown are weighted joint generalized least squares estimates, with before-tax total compensation of the worker-group serving as the weight. Weighting is used to correct for possible heteroscedasticity, although unweighted joint GLS results are qualitatively similar.

1. *Relations Between Control Variables and Fringe Benefit Shares.* We turn first to the coefficients of the control variables; that is, the x_ks. These appear under the headings "Variables in the Pension Equation" and "Variables in the Health Insurance Equation" of table 3.5.

The first five variables shown—average schooling, proportion of workers female, proportion of workers white, and proportion of work-

Table 3.4   Descriptive Statistics of Variables
in the EEEC Survey Data

Variable	Mean	Standard Deviation	Minimum	Maximum
Variables from imputed tax rates, individual shares:				
s_w (wage share)	0.916	0.061	0.644	1.0
s_r (pension share)	0.041	0.044	0.0	0.279
s_h (health insurance share)	0.043	0.029	0.0	0.297
p_r/p_w	0.742	0.077	0.300	0.990
p_h/p_w	0.762	0.109	0.267	1.274
m/P^* (real total compensation, $)	8,959	3,350	389	23,896
m'/P^* (instrument for real total compensation, $)	8,877	3,121	415	22,568
Variables from imputed tax rates, household shares:				
s_w (wage share)	0.940	0.048	0.709	1.0
s_r (pension share)	0.030	0.033	0.0	0.199
s_h (health insurance share)	0.030	0.022	0.0	0.223
p_r/p_w	0.742	0.077	0.300	0.990
p_h/p_w	0.762	0.109	0.267	1.274
m/P^* (real total compensation, $)	12,826	3,912	830	32,512
m'/P^* (instrument for real total compensation, $)	12,761	3,716	863	33,592
Variables from direct tax rates, individual shares:				
s_w (wage share)	0.915	0.062	0.644	1.0
s_r (pension share)	0.042	0.044	0.0	0.279
s_h (health insurance share)	0.043	0.029	0.0	0.306
p_r/p_w	0.799	0.046	0.619	0.993
p_h/p_w	0.820	0.094	0.502	1.120
m/P^* (real total compensation, $)	9,572	3,834	384	39,002
m'/P^* (instrument for real total compensation, $)	9,482	3,597	410	40,509

Table 3.4 (continued)

Variable	Mean	Standard Deviation	Minimum	Maximum
Variables from direct tax rates, household shares:				
s_w (wage share)	0.939	0.049	0.704	1.0
s_r (pension share)	0.030	0.034	0.0	0.199
s_h (health insurance share)	0.031	0.023	0.0	0.231
p_r/p_w	0.799	0.046	0.619	0.993
p_h/p_w	0.820	0.094	0.502	1.120
m/P^* (real total compensation, $)	13,794	4,931	819	60,356
m'/P^* (instrument for real total compensation, $)	13,721	4,745	852	61,856
Variables common to all computations:				
Average schooling	12.08	1.40	7.64	18.00
Proportion of workers female	0.352	0.227	0.0	1.0
Proportion of workers white	0.915	0.081	0.0	1.0
Proportion workers younger than 30	0.348	0.120	0.0	1.0
Proportion workers older than 50	0.224	0.081	0.0	1.0
Number of employees per establishment	737.71	1,745.02	1.0	22,263
Union contract	0.206	0.404	0.0	1.0
White-collar worker-group	0.514	0.500	0.0	1.0
Establishment located in an SMSA	0.741	0.438	0.0	1.0
Establishment located in:				
Northeast	0.258	0.437	0.0	1.0
South	0.258	0.438	0.0	1.0
West	0.154	0.361	0.0	1.0
Still proxy	0.076	0.038	0.0	0.263
Part-time workers	1.081	0.251	0.177	7.247

NOTES: The sample is composed of 5,234 observations on groups of workers in 3,320 establishments in the U.S. in 1977. Worker-groups are of either blue-collar workers (that is, nonoffice workers) or white-collar (office) workers. EEEC worker-group data are supplemented with data from the Current Population Survey and National Medical Care Expenditure Survey (see text).

Table 3.5 Estimated Coefficients of the Fringe Benefit Demand System Applied to the EEEC Survey Data

Parameter or Variable	Imputed Tax Rates		Direct Tax Rates	
	Individual Shares	Household Shares	Individual Shares	Household Shares
a_w	1.7650	1.4331	1.4903	1.3151
	$(-)$	$(-)$	$(-)$	$(-)$
a_r	-0.5878	-0.3408	-0.4643	-0.3124
	(0.0420)	(0.0354)	(0.0325)	(0.0273)
a_h	-0.1772	-0.0923	-0.0260	-0.0027
	(0.0255)	(0.0212)	(0.0200)	(0.0166)
b_{ww}	-0.0488	-0.0540	-0.1077	-0.0690
	$(-)$	$(-)$	$(-)$	$(-)$
b_{wr}	0.0609	0.0553	0.0799	0.0481
	$(-)$	$(-)$	$(-)$	$(-)$
b_{wh}	-0.0121	-0.0013	0.0278	0.0209
	$(-)$	$(-)$	$(-)$	$(-)$
b_{rr}	-0.0766	-0.0618	-0.0680	-0.0392
	(0.0128)	(0.0100)	(0.0148)	(0.0117)
b_{rh}	0.0157	0.0065	-0.0119	-0.0089
	(0.0087)	(0.0068)	(0.0092)	(0.0072)
b_{hh}	-0.0036	-0.0052	-0.0159	-0.0120
	(0.0079)	(0.0060)	(0.0081)	(0.0062)
b_w	-0.0971	-0.0582	-0.0667	-0.0456
	$(-)$	$(-)$	$(-)$	$(-)$
b_r	0.0680	0.0401	0.0546	0.0374
	(0.0044)	(0.0037)	(0.0031)	(0.0026)
b_h	0.0291	0.0181	0.0121	0.0082
	(0.0026)	(0.0022)	(0.0019)	(0.0016)
Variables in the Pension Equation:				
Average schooling	0.0020	0.0025	0.0029	0.0031
	(0.0011)	(0.0009)	(0.0012)	(0.0009)
Proportion of workers female	0.0621	-0.0083	0.0503	-0.0110
	(0.0057)	(0.0039)	(0.0049)	(0.0039)
Proportion of workers white	0.0194	0.0066	0.0212	0.0080
	(0.0103)	(0.0083)	(0.0105)	(0.0084)
Proportion of workers younger than 30	-0.0284	-0.0204	-0.0369	-0.0268
	(0.0077)	(0.0062)	(0.0078)	(0.0062)
Proportion of workers older than 50	0.0057	-0.0003	0.0055	0.0005
	(0.0103)	(0.0082)	(0.0104)	(0.0083)

Table 3.5 (*continued*)

Parameter or Variable	Imputed Tax Rates		Direct Tax Rates	
	Individual Shares	Household Shares	Individual Shares	Household Shares
Number of employees per establishment (1,000s)	0.0008 (0.0001)	0.0008 (0.0001)	0.0008 (0.0001)	0.0008 (0.0001)
Union contract	0.0002 (0.0013)	−0.0006 (0.0010)	−0.0004 (0.0013)	−0.0011 (0.0010)
White-collar workers	−0.0175 (0.0033)	−0.0081 (0.0026)	−0.0177 (0.0033)	−0.0090 (0.0026)
Establishment located in an SMSA	−0.0019 (0.0019)	0.0007 (0.0015)	0.0011 (0.0019)	0.0024 (0.0015)
Establishment located in:				
Northeast	0.0169 (0.0012)	0.0161 (0.0010)	0.0160 (0.0013)	0.0153 (0.0010)
South	0.0049 (0.0019)	−0.0012 (0.0015)	0.0004 (0.0020)	−0.0034 (0.0015)
West	0.0002 (0.0015)	−0.0024 (0.0012)	−0.0002 (0.0016)	−0.0023 (0.0012)
Skill proxy	0.3824 (0.0215)	0.3123 (0.0171)	0.4064 (0.0217)	0.3254 (0.0173)
Part-time workers	−0.0578 (0.0037)	−0.0431 (0.0029)	−0.0588 (0.0037)	−0.0434 (0.0030)
Variables in the Health Insurance Equation:				
Average schooling	0.0018 (0.0007)	0.0020 (0.0005)	0.0022 (0.0007)	0.0022 (0.0006)
Proportion of workers female	0.0248 (0.0035)	−0.0144 (0.0024)	0.0101 (0.0030)	−0.0178 (0.0024)
Proportion of workers white	−0.0120 (0.0063)	−0.0185 (0.0050)	−0.0092 (0.0064)	−0.0152 (0.0051)
Proportion of workers younger than 30	0.0078 (0.0047)	0.0111 (0.0037)	0.0030 (0.0048)	0.0071 (0.0038)
Proportion of workers older than 50	−0.0121 (0.0063)	−0.0083 (0.0049)	−0.0143 (0.0064)	−0.0091 (0.0050)
Number of employees per establishment (1000s)	−0.0005 (0.0001)	−0.0003 (0.0001)	−0.0005 (0.0001)	−0.0003 (0.0001)
Union contract	0.0079 (0.0008)	0.0055 (0.0006)	0.0075 (0.0008)	0.0053 (0.0006)
White-collar workers	−0.0185 (0.0020)	−0.0109 (0.0016)	−0.0179 (0.0020)	−0.0112 (0.0016)

Table 3.5 (*continued*)

Parameter or Variable	Imputed Tax Rates		Direct Tax Rates	
	Individual Shares	Household Shares	Individual Shares	Household Shares
Establishment located	-0.0004	0.0008	0.0009	0.0014
in an SMSA	(0.0013)	(0.0010)	(0.0013)	(0.0011)
Establishment located in:				
Northeast	-0.0022	-0.0006	-0.0031	-0.0015
	(0.0008)	(0.0006)	(0.0008)	(0.0006)
South	-0.0051	-0.0065	-0.0076	-0.0077
	(0.0014)	(0.0011)	(0.0014)	(0.0011)
West	0.0015	-0.0002	0.0006	-0.0005
	(0.0009)	(0.0007)	(0.0010)	(0.0008)
Skill proxy	0.1792	0.1482	0.1973	0.1595
	(0.0132)	(0.0104)	(0.0133)	(0.0105)
Part-time workers	-0.0377	-0.0294	-0.0390	-0.0299
	(0.0022)	(0.0018)	(0.0023)	(0.0018)
Mean squared error				
(system)	0.9999	0.9999	1.0003	1.0001
R-squared (system)	0.5332	0.5688	0.5268	0.5680

NOTES: Estimates result from applying an iterative weighted version of Zellner's seemingly unrelated regression procedure to equations (2.34) and (2.35). Before-tax total compensation is the weight used. "Imputed Tax Rates" indicates that marginal tax rates (and the implied tax-price of wages) were imputed from information contained in the federal tax codes. "Direct Tax Rates" indicates that marginal tax rates were assigned directly to each observation from *Statistics of Income* based on gross household income.

The dependent variables are the shares of total compensation received as pensions and as health insurance. "Individual Shares" denotes use of equation (3.1) to compute compensation shares; "Household Shares" denotes use of equation (3.2).

Asymptotic standard error of each coefficient is shown in parentheses. Parameters computed from restrictions placed on the model are indicated by (-).

Coefficients of the nonprice variables (shown under "Variables in the Pension Equation" and "Variables in the Health Equation") are interpretable simply as the change in the share of total compensation received as pension benefits (or as health insurance benefits) resulting from a unit change in the independent variable, all else equal.

Each equation includes a set of two-digit industry dummy variables, in addition to the control variables shown.

ers younger than 30 and older than 50 — were appended to each EEEC worker-group record from the CPS. The schooling and age variables are related in a straightforward way to fringe benefit shares. Worker-groups with greater schooling receive a greater share of total compensation as both pensions and health insurance; a one-year increase in a group's average schooling adds .2 or .3 percentage point to the share of compensation received as pensions, and adds .2 percentage point to the share received as health insurance. Young worker-groups receive a smaller proportion of their total compensation as pensions; a group of workers composed entirely of workers under 30 would receive 2 or 3 percentage points less of its total compensation as pensions than would a group composed entirely of workers over 30. But *older* worker-groups receive a smaller proportion of their compensation as *health insurance*; a group of workers, all of whom were over 50, would receive about 1 percentage point less of its compensation as health insurance than would another group, all of whom were under 50.

The relation between race and fringe benefit shares is relatively weak. If a larger proportion of a worker-group is white, that group may receive a slightly larger share of compensation as pensions, and a slightly smaller share of compensation as health insurance.

The effect of the proportion of workers who are female differs dramatically depending on whether individual or household shares are used as the dependent variable. When individual shares are used as the dependent variable, the results suggest that a higher proportion of women increases fringe benefit shares, as has been found in several previous investigations, including ours (above) using the NIPA. But when household shares are used as the dependent variable, the opposite is found: A higher proportion of women lowers fringe benefit shares, as would be suggested by the reasoning that women tend to rely on the pension and health insurance benefits of their spouses. This finding is useful because it backs up the interpretation that has been given to the often-found positive relation between the proportion of women in a group and the provision of fringe benefits: that fringe benefits are frequently a fixed sum per worker, and hence a larger share of the compensation of women, whose total compensation tends to be lower than men's. This interpretation would seem to be correct. As the findings in table 3.5 show, the positive relation between women and fringe benefits disappears when household shares of total compensation are used as the dependent variable. Hence, the frequent finding that a higher proportion of women increases fringe benefits would seem to be a result of using individual worker shares of total compensation as the dependent variable. When a more appropriate household measure of the share of fringe benefits is adopted, a more plausible negative relation emerges.

Establishment size appears to have an effect on fringe benefit shares that is statistically significantly different from zero, but quite small. For every additional 1,000 workers, establishments pay about .1 percentage point more in pensions and .05 percentage point less in health insurance. These findings relating establishment size to fringe benefit shares are discussed further below.

The results in table 3.5 suggest a much smaller effect of collective bargaining on fringe benefit provision than earlier studies using the EEEC. For example, both Freeman (1981) and Alpert (1983) used EEEC data and found that unions shift the mix of compensation toward fringe benefits. But the table 3.5 results suggest that coverage by a collective bargaining contract is unrelated to the pension share of compensation, and has only a small effect on the health insurance share. (Collective bargaining increases the health insurance share of compensation by about .5 percentage point.)

Several factors may explain the differences between the table 3.5 results on unions and the findings of Freeman and Alpert on unions and fringe benefits. For example, Freeman (1981) did not attempt to control for the marginal tax rate facing each group of workers. Moreover, Alpert (1983), who did control for marginal tax rates, found the union effect on fringe benefits to be strongly interdependent with industrial concentration and the specific human capital of a group of workers.

It is true that excluding certain variables from the equations reported in table 3.5 would lead to larger union impacts. To the extent that industry and occupation are correlated with unionism, the industry dummy variables and the white-collar dummy variable undoubtedly reduce the size of the union coefficient. Note, for example, that white-collar workers, who tend to be nonunion, receive a smaller share of their compensation as pensions and health insurance than do blue-collar workers. But if any single conclusion can be drawn from the enormous existing body of research on union effects, it is that the net independent impact of collective bargaining is extremely difficult to pin down. Perhaps the safest conclusion to draw from table 3.5 is that once all of the factors determining the demand for fringe benefits are adequately controlled for, the net independent impact of unions and collective bargaining on the mix of compensation is rather small.[15]

Independent of their influence on health insurance prices, location, and region do not appear to be important determinants of the compensation mix. Location in an SMSA is unrelated to either pensions or health insurance. Workers in the northeast do receive a larger share of compensation as pensions (about 1.5 percentage points more), and workers in the south receive a smaller share of compensation as health insurance (about .5 percentage point less). But no other regional impacts appear in these results.

Greater skill, as approximated by the ratio of paid leave hours to total hours worked, has a large impact on the mix of compensation. A 1 percentage point increase in the ratio of paid leave hours to total hours worked (say, from 7 to 8 percent of total hours) is related to a 3 to 4 percentage point increase in the pension share of compensation, and to a 1.5 to 2 percentage point increase in the health insurance share of compensation. In that the skill proxy's influence on deferred compensation (that is, pensions) is greater than its influence on current compensation (health insurance), these results again provide evidence in favor of the agency hypothesis.[16]

A greater proportion of part-time workers in a worker-group depresses both the pension and health insurance shares of compensation. An increase in the ratio of the total workers (full-time and part-time) to full-time equivalent workers from 1 to 2 would reduce the pension share of compensation by 4 to 6 percentage points, and reduce the health insurance share of compensation by 3 to 4 percentage points. Although statistically different from zero, this relation is less strong than might be expected. For example, it implies that if a group of 50 full-time workers became a group of 100 half-time workers, the share of their compensation received as fringe benefits would fall by only 4 or 5 percentage points. The implication is that even voluntarily provided pensions and health insurance are an important fixed cost of employing workers, whether part-time or full-time.

In order to conserve space, we do not report the coefficients of the 50 included two-digit industry dummy variables, but offer a brief summary of these findings in a footnote.[17]

2. *Price, Income, and Substitution Elasticities.* The parameters shown in table 3.5 can be transformed into compensated price elasticities (η_{ij}^*), uncompensated price elasticities (η_{ij}), income elasticities (η_{im}), and elasticities of substitution (σ_{ij}). These elasticities, all computed at the sample mean, are displayed in table 3.6, and the standard error of each elasticity is shown in parentheses below each elasticity. (See chapter 2 for a discussion of how these standard errors were computed.) The elasticities displayed in the four columns of table 3.6 correspond to the parameter estimates given in the four columns of table 3.5.

As noted in the discussion of the NIPA data, the compensated and uncompensated price elasticities (η_{ij}^*, and η_{ij}) can be derived by the Slutsky equation from the compensation shares, the income elasticities (η_{im}), and the elasticities of substitution (σ_{ij}). Hence, it is again useful to focus on the latter two elasticities.

The estimated income elasticities of demand for wages, pensions, and health insurance (η_{im}) are similar in each of the four estimated equation systems. As was true in the NIPA data, there is again strong evidence that the demand for wage benefits is income inelastic, with a point estimate of η_{wm} in the range of 0.90 to 0.95. Also in accord with the NIPA estimates, these results suggest that the demand for both pensions and health insurance is income elastic. For pensions, the income elasticity of demand for pensions is around 1.6. For health insurance, the income elasticity is somewhat lower, around 1.2 to 1.5. Note that the income elasticities of demand for both pensions and health insurance are statistically significantly greater than unity at roughly the 5-percent level using a two-tailed test. Hence, the income elasticity estimates from the EEEC tend to confirm the conclusion reached earlier that the growth of pensions during the post-World War II years cannot be explained by rising marginal income tax rates alone.

The degree of uniformity exhibited by the four different estimated elasticities of substitution (σ_{ij}) is less in the case of the EEEC than was true with the NIPA data. Nevertheless, the EEEC elasticity estimates accord in general with the NIPA estimates reported above. Specifically, the EEEC estimates tend to confirm that pensions and health insurance benefits both substitute for wages, and that pensions and wages are probably better substitutes than health benefits and wages. In the EEEC, the evidence is stronger than in the NIPA data that σ_{wr} exceeds unity. But again the evidence suggests that σ_{wh} is probably insignificantly different from unity. Although we can again conclude with some confidence that both pensions and health insurance are substitutes for wages, we must again be more tentative in concluding that the possibilities for substitution between wages and health insurance are great.

The estimated elasticity of substitution between pensions and health insurance (σ_{rh}) is never statistically significantly different from zero, but the point estimates range between 3 to 4 when imputed tax rates are used, and between -1 and -2 when direct tax rates are used. Hence, there is only weak evidence to support the notion, suggested rather weakly by the NIPA estimates, that pensions and health insurance are complements.

Comparative Discussion

The two empirical investigations—one using the NIPA data and the other using the EEEC survey data—have offered many results that are in accord and a few that conflict. The most important results pertain to the effects of income and prices (or taxes) on the mix of compensation, and on these points the two data sets offer strikingly similar implications.

Table 3.6   Price, Income, and Substitution Elasticities
Computed from Fringe Benefit Demand System
Applied to the EEEC Survey Data

	Imputed Tax Rates		Direct Tax Rates	
	Individual Shares	Household Shares	Individual Shares	Household Shares
Compensated Price Elasticities:				
η^*_{ww}	-0.20	-0.17	-0.28	-0.19
	(0.07)	(0.05)	(0.05)	(0.07)
η^*_{rr}	-1.78	-1.85	-1.68	-1.52
	(0.50)	(0.52)	(0.37)	(0.46)
η^*_{hh}	-1.00	-1.07	-1.21	-1.22
	(0.15)	(0.16)	(0.21)	(0.21)
η^*_{wr}	0.16	0.13	0.18	0.12
	(0.05)	(0.04)	(0.04)	(0.05)
η^*_{rw}	1.55	1.72	1.76	1.59
	(0.42)	(0.47)	(0.43)	(0.52)
η^*_{wh}	0.04	0.04	0.09	0.07
	(0.03)	(0.02)	(0.02)	(0.03)
η^*_{hw}	0.65	0.85	1.31	1.35
	(0.12)	(0.11)	(0.30)	(0.30)
η^*_{rh}	0.23	0.14	-0.07	-0.09
	(0.13)	(0.11)	(0.13)	(0.13)
η^*_{hr}	0.35	0.21	-0.11	-0.13
	(0.19)	(0.16)	(0.20)	(0.20)
Uncompensated Price Elasticities:				
η_{ww}	-0.96	-1.00	-1.06	-1.03
	(0.02)	(0.01)	(0.02)	(0.02)
η_{rr}	-1.94	-1.96	-1.82	-1.62
	(0.46)	(0.48)	(0.34)	(0.42)
η_{hh}	-1.09	-1.13	-1.28	-1.27
	(0.14)	(0.15)	(0.19)	(0.19)
η_{wr}	0.08	0.07	0.10	0.06
	(0.02)	(0.01)	(0.01)	(0.02)
η_{rw}	0.03	0.30	0.38	0.22
	(0.15)	(0.20)	(0.19)	(0.22)
η_{wh}	-0.01	0.00	0.04	0.03
	(0.01)	(0.01)	(0.01)	(0.01)
η_{hw}	-0.63	-0.39	0.29	0.30
	(0.36)	(0.25)	(0.20)	(0.19)

Table 3.6 (*continued*)

	Imputed Tax Rates		Direct Tax Rates	
	Individual Shares	Household Shares	Individual Shares	Household Shares
η_{rh}	0.13	0.07	-0.17	-0.16
	(0.13)	(0.11)	(0.13)	(0.13)
η_{hr}	0.22	0.12	-0.22	-0.21
	(0.19)	(0.16)	(0.19)	(0.19)
Income Elasticities:				
η_{wm}	0.89	0.93	0.92	0.95
	(0.01)	(0.01)	(0.01)	(0.01)
η_{rm}	1.78	1.60	1.62	1.55
	(0.39)	(0.30)	(0.28)	(0.31)
η_{hm}	1.50	1.40	1.20	1.18
	(0.25)	(0.21)	(0.10)	(0.10)
Elasticities of Substitution:				
σ_{wr}	1.81	1.93	2.06	1.80
	(0.38)	(0.44)	(0.40)	(0.49)
σ_{wh}	0.76	0.97	1.55	1.52
	(0.16)	(0.11)	(0.28)	(0.28)
σ_{rh}	4.06	3.16	-1.26	-1.91
	(3.04)	(2.91)	(3.40)	(2.55)
Sample Mean Shares:				
s_w	0.916	0.940	0.915	0.939
s_r	0.041	0.030	0.042	0.030
s_h	0.043	0.030	0.043	0.031

NOTES: Elasticities computed from the parameter estimates displayed in table 3.5. (See chapter 2 for a discussion of the elasticities and details of their computation.) Standard error of each elasticity is in parentheses below each elasticity. (Standard errors are computed by taking a Taylor approximation at the sample mean.)

These findings can be summarized as follows.

(a) The findings from both data sets indicate that the demand for wage benefits is income inelastic, whereas the demand for pensions and health insurance is income elastic. Hence, a doubling of total compensation would result in less than a doubling of wage benefits, whereas the same doubling of income would substantially more than double pension and health insurance benefits.

(b) The findings from both data sets indicate that both pensions and health insurance are good substitutes for wage benefits, and that pensions are probably a better substitute for wages than health insurance. (We infer that pensions are a better substitute for wages than health insurance from the point estimates rather than from formal statistical tests.)

(c) Evidence on whether pensions and health insurance are substitutes or complements is relatively weak. Findings from both data sets suggest that pensions and health insurance may be complements, but in no case do statistical tests offer a rejection of the hypothesis that the elasticity of substitution between pensions and health insurance is zero. Hence, it is safest to conclude that pensions and health insurance are separable in consumption.

It is important that the two separate investigations offer similar results about the effects of income and prices on the mix of total compensation, because these are the fringe benefit determinants that have changed most over the last 20 years. Demographic changes, however inexorable, have been more gradual. Moreover, it is through the income and price effects that changes in tax policy have made their mark on the mix of total compensation. The sensitivity of compensation shares to changes in tax policy will become clearer in the next chapter, where simulations of various tax policy changes are presented.

The two empirical analyses are in somewhat less agreement on the effects of other variables on the mix of compensation. Undoubtedly, part of the problem here is that whatever control variables were at hand were used in each investigation. The lack of uniformity between the two data sets in available control variables could itself lead to important differences in the measured effects of included variables. Nevertheless, several findings in common emerge, and these can be summarized as follows.

(a) Older workers tend to receive a greater share of compensation as pensions, other things equal. The two data sets are in conflict, and hence yield no conclusive finding, on whether older workers receive more or less health insurance, other things equal.

(b) Blue-collar workers tend to receive a greater share of compensation as pensions, other things equal. But again, the two data sets conflict on whether blue-collar workers receive more or less health insurance.

(c) Greater firm-specific skill increases the pension share of total compensation, and has a greater positive effect on pensions than on health insurance. This finding strongly supports the agency hypothesis that employers use deferred compensation, such as pensions, to create a bond between the firm and workers who have skills that can be acquired only through tenure with the firm.

(d) When the unit of observation is properly defined as the household — as is done in the investigation using the EEEC survey — it can be seen that women receive a smaller share of their compensation as both pensions and health insurance, other things equal. This suggests that women tend to rely on the fringe benefits of their spouses and may also suggest discrimination in compensation.

(e) The findings about the effects of establishment size on the mix of compensation are rather weak. This is in contrast to the findings of many previous studies but accords with results reported in Hamermesh and Woodbury (1990). Results from the NIPA data suggest that larger establishments provide a smaller share of compensation as pensions, whereas the EEEC survey results suggest that larger establishments provide a slightly larger share of compensation as pensions. Regarding health insurance provision, results from the NIPA data suggest no relationship between establishment size and provision of health benefits, whereas the EEEC survey suggests a very slight negative effect of establishment size on health benefits. Interpreting the relationship between establishment size and fringe benefit provision is a difficult matter because many factors may be associated with establishment size — industry concentration, the need to monitor and regiment the workforce, and economies of scale (Mellow 1983). It is usually supposed that larger groups of workers are able to take advantage of scale economies in the provision of fringe benefits — especially health and life insurance — but the results reported here offer only weak support for such a hypothesis. Rather, our results suggest that establishment size plays a limited role in the provision of fringe benefits, which suggests in turn that the positive relationships between establishment size and fringe benefit provision found in previous studies may be the result of an inability to control fully for income, tax-price, and other effects.

In completing this comparative discussion, it is useful to examine the industry composition of the two samples used. Table 3.7 displays, for each of the two samples, the percentage of employment accounted for by each industry, and the percentage of establishments (for the NIPA) or worker-groups (for the EEEC) accounted for by each industry. The NIPA percentages can be thought of as population percentages, since the NIPA attempt to account for all private economic activity that takes place in the nation. How closely the EEEC percentages correspond to the NIPA percentages can give an idea of how representative is the EEEC survey.

Table 3.7 suggests that manufacturing (especially durable goods manufacturing) and utilities are overrepresented in the EEEC survey, and that construction, retail trades, services, and agriculture (the only evident omission) are underrepresented. This is not surprising in that the EEEC survey is a stratified random sample, as any nationally representative survey of establishments must be in order to yield reliable inferences about the population of establishments. Stratification implies oversampling establishments in industries that have relatively few, but large, establishments (such as manufacturing and utilities), and consequently implies undersampling establishments in industries that have many small establishments (such as construction, retail trade, and services).

That the EEEC survey drew establishments from all segments of the private economy (except agriculture) makes the similarities between the two empirical analyses presented above somewhat less surprising than might otherwise be the case. But there remain basic differences between the two data sets. The NIPA data set used in estimation is a pooled time-series of cross sections from 1968 through 1982, with the two-digit industry as the unit of observation. The EEEC survey is a cross section

**Table 3.7 Comparison of NIPA and 1977 EEEC Survey Samples:
Percentages of Employment and Establishments
(or Worker-Groups) Accounted for by Each Industry**

Industry	Percentage of Employment		Percentage of Establishments or Worker-Groups	
	NIPA	**EEEC**	**NIPA**	**EEEC**
Agriculture	0.40	0	1.12	0
Mining	1.23	1.82	0.66	1.58
Construction	5.84	1.06	10.94	5.33
Manufacturing				
Durable	17.98	34.07	4.63	21.53
Nondurable	12.24	12.94	3.30	14.98
Transportation	3.46	1.69	3.13	3.67
Communication	3.77	6.07	1.18	1.22
Utilities	1.07	9.40	0.38	2.43
Wholesale Trade	7.06	1.27	9.20	8.20
Retail Trade	20.98	6.72	31.21	17.62
Finance, Insurance,				
Real Estate	7.36	11.83	10.26	6.74
Services	18.61	13.13	23.98	16.70

NOTES: Agriculture excludes farms, and hence includes only agricultural services, forestry, and fisheries. Transportation excludes railroads. National Income and Product Accounts data are for 1977. In the National Income and Product Accounts data, total full-time equivalent employment in the industries listed was 61.1 million, and there were a total of 4.01 million establishments accounted for (see U.S. Department of Commerce, Bureau of the Census, *County Business Patterns*). In the 1977 EEEC survey, 2.12 million workers were employed in the 5,234 worker-groups used in estimation.

of establishments in 1977. Nevertheless, differences between the two data sets in industry composition cannot explain the remaining relatively minor differences between the two sets of results.

Appendix to Chapter 3
A Hedonic Price Index of Health Insurance

This appendix develops the measure of the employer's cost of health insurance (c_h) that is used with both the National Income and Product Accounts (NIPA) data and the 1977 EEEC survey in this chapter. Recall that in the empirical work using the NIPA data, variation over time in the cost of health insurance (c_h) was measured by observing the health insurance price index published in the NIPA (U.S. Department of Commerce, Bureau of Economic Analysis, 1986, Table 7.10). There is no ready source of data on industry-to-industry variations in health insurance costs, however. The solution adopted here is to estimate a so-called hedonic model of the cost of health insurance, and to construct an index of health insurance price based on that model. It is worth noting at the outset that only one set of interindustry price differentials is computed in the work presented here. When applied to the NIPA data for 1968 through 1982, this set of interindustry cost differentials is assumed to be constant over the 15 years in question.

Basically, the hedonic approach is a way of estimating how changes in the quality of a good affect the price of that good. For example, automobiles are sold in many varieties with many different options, and it would be interesting to know how different options affect the price of an automobile. Zvi Griliches (1971) has applied the hedonic approach to precisely this case. He regresses the price of an automobile (P_a) on the various characteristics of the automobile ($Char_1$, $Char_2$, ..., $Char_N$):

$$P_a = f_0 + f_1 Char_1 + f_2 Char_2 + \ldots + f_N Char_N + e. \qquad (3.3)$$

In equation (3.3), $Char_1$ might be the horsepower of the engine, $Char_2$ the shipping weight in pounds, and so on. (Griliches includes a constant term, f_0, and a random error term (e) in the equation.) Ordinary least squares estimation of equation (3.3) yields estimates of the coefficients ($f_1, f_2, \ldots, f_N$), each of which provides an estimate of the change in the price of an automobile that would accompany a change in the associated characteristic. For example, Griliches used 1960 data and found that an increase of 10 units of horsepower would on average result in a 1.2 percent increase in the price of a car, other things equal.

The same basic idea may be applied to health insurance. Health insurance is a highly heterogeneous good, and different premiums are charged for health insurance plans that have different features. If we could observe the premiums paid for many individual primary health insurance holders *and* the characteristics of the health insurance plans purchased, then we could estimate a hedonic equation for the price of health insurance patterned after (3.3). Specifically, we could regress the annual premium (*Prem*) on the characteristics of the health insurance plan:

$$Prem = f_0 + f_1 Char_1 + f_2 Char_2 + \ldots + f_N Char_N + e. \qquad (3.4)$$

In equation (3.4), the variables $Char_1$, $Char_2$, $\ldots$, $Char_N$, now refer to the features of the health insurance plan. These would include, for example, the deductible (the flat payment that must be paid before the insurance covers medical care charges), the coinsurance rate (the fraction of the price of medical services that the insurance pays for), and any limits or maximums on reimbursement to the policyholder for medical care received. Each of the coefficients (f_1, f_2, $\ldots$, f_N) in equation (3.4) provides an estimate of the change in the health insurance premium that would accompany a change in the associated characteristic of the health insurance plan.

Our main interest, however, is in obtaining estimates of how health insurance costs vary from industry to industry. To obtain such estimates, we could add to equation (3.4) variables that capture the industry in which the insured individual works. Making such a modification, we would have:

$$Prem = f_0 + f_1 Char_1 + f_2 Char_2 + \ldots + f_N Char_N + \qquad (3.5)$$
$$v_1 Ind_1 + v_2 Ind_2 + \ldots + v_N Ind_N + e.$$

In equation (3.5), Ind_1 would equal one if the insured individual worked in industry 1 (zero otherwise), Ind_2 would equal one if the insured individual worked in industry 2, and so on. The coefficients of these industry dummy variables can be interpreted as the health insurance cost differentials faced by firms in each industry, other things equal. That is, the coefficient of Ind_1 shows the amount by which the cost to an employer in industry 1 of providing a standardized health insurance plan deviates from a norm. These coefficients, then, provide the basis for a health insurance cost index.

The hedonic health insurance price function (eq. 3.5) can be estimated using a unique data base that became available only in 1987. The National Medical Care Expenditure Survey (NMCES) is a 1977–78 survey of roughly 14,000 households that was designed to obtain data on the health status, access to health care, and health insurance coverage of a representative sample of the civilian, noninstitutional U.S. population. The NMCES is in two parts. The first part—a household survey—contains standard demographic data, as well as the data on health status and access to health care that were the primary reasons for conducting the survey (Kasper, Walden, and Wilson 1983). The second part—the Health Insurance/Employer Survey—is a supplement to the NMCES that includes data obtained *from employers* on (a) premiums paid for the health insurance of each covered worker in the sample, and (b) the benefits available and services covered under each health insurance plan (Cantor 1986).

In order to obtain the hedonic health insurance price function, we created a sample of approximately 5,000 private sector workers who were covered by health insurance and for whom complete information on premiums and benefits were available. The hedonic function estimated differed depending on whether the price index being created was to be matched with the NIPA data, or with the 1977 EEEC survey data.

To obtain the price index that is matched with the NIPA data, estimating the hedonic function (3.5) involves regressing the health insurance premium paid for each worker on the characteristics of the health insurance plan, a vector of individual characteristics, and a set of industry dummy variables. Appendix table A3.1 displays the estimated coefficients of the industry dummy variables.

The individual characteristics included in the equation are age, age-squared, and dummy variables for female, white, black, and Hispanic origin. Note that including the individual characteristics is necessary in

Table A3.1 Hedonic Price Function for Health Insurance: Estimates Used with the NIPA Data

Independent Variable	Mean (Sample Proportion)	OLS Coefficient (Standard Error)
Agriculture	0.011	-82.28
		(65.10)
Mining	0.017	112.33
		(56.66)
Construction	0.036	51.24
		(39.06)
Manufacturing	0.228	54.11
		(20.72)
Transportation, Communication, Utilities	0.073	83.69
		(29.25)
Sales	0.118	-22.96
		(24.73)
Finance, Insurance, Real Estate	0.051	14.41
		(33.46)
Services (Repair)	0.043	-11.27
		(35.82)
Services (Personal)	0.011	-18.30
		(67.30)
Services (Entertainment)	0.007	-75.69
		(84.24)
Services (Professional)	0.117	12.54
		(24.66)
Other or Unknown Industry	0.288	Omitted category
R-squared (adjusted)		0.302
F-ratio		48.888

NOTES: The equation estimated is an ordinary least squares regression of the primary insured's total annual group health insurance premium on the variables shown in the table, a set of independent variables characterizing the health insurance package (see the text), and the following additional independent variables: age, age-squared, and dummy variables for female, white, black, and Hispanic origin. The mean of the dependent variable (the annual health insurance premium) is $829.74 (with a standard deviation of $552.33). A sample of 4,764 individuals from the 1977–78 National Medical Care Expenditure Survey was used to estimate the equation.

order for the coefficients of the industry dummies to be uncontaminated by the characteristics of each industry's workforce. The characteristics of the health insurance plan included in the equation are as follows: (a) a set of dummy variables characterizing type of coverage (covered by basic benefits only, covered by both major medical and basic benefits); (b) a set of dummy variables indicating the number of individuals covered by the plan (coverage of only the primary-insured worker, coverage of the primary-insured worker and one additional person, coverage of all family members); (c) a set of variables indicating the generosity of major medical benefits (the major medical coinsurance rate, a dummy variable equal to one if out-of-pocket expenses from part of a prior deductible period can be applied to the current deductible period, a dummy variable equal to one if the maximum amount payable out-of-pocket by the insured for major medical is $750 or less, a dummy variable equal to one if there is no limit on the amount payable out-of-pocket by the insured); (d) a set of variables indicating breadth of coverage (coverage for services related to pregnancy, coverage for vision care, coverage for hearing exams, coverage for a routine physical examination, coverage for physician office services, and the deductible for physician office services); (e) a set of variables characterizing the psychiatric services covered (coverage for outpatient psychiatric care, and whether the outpatient psychiatric services for diagnosis are the same as for general outpatient benefits); (f) a set of dummy variables indicating the generosity of hospital benefits (hospital benefits generous and no deductible, hospital benefits generous but there is a deductible, hospital benefits less generous and there is a deductible)[18]; (g) a dummy variable equal to one if a second opinion is required before inpatient surgery; and (h) a set of variables characterizing the outpatient services covered (whether outpatient hospital services are covered, whether outpatient diagnostic procedures such as X-ray and laboratory tests are covered, and the deductible for outpatient diagnostic services). Several of these variables are similar to those used by Wilensky, Farley, and Taylor (1984) to describe the coverage provided by health insurance plans using the NMCES data. It should be clear that these variables provide a comprehensive profile of the health insurance plan that covered each primary-insured worker in the sample.

The estimates in table A3.1 suggest that health insurance costs are relatively high in mining, transportation, and manufacturing, and relatively low in sales and services generally (as well as agriculture). The findings accord with the idea that industries in which jobs pose greater hazards to health are the industries in which health insurance costs tend to be high. Recall that these estimates control for both the individual characteristics of the primary-insured worker and the characteristics of the health insurance package, so that the relatively low health insurance costs in sales cannot be explained, for example, by the overrepresentation in that industry of women who are provided relatively meager health benefits. Rather, the coefficients provide a "pure" estimate of the cost to employers in each industry of a standardized package of health insurance benefits.

The coefficients displayed in table A3.1 can be converted into a price index by the following procedure. First, evaluate the health insurance premium at the mean of all the independent variables excluding the industry dummy variables. Call this *Prem'*. Then divide each industry coefficient by *Prem'* and add one to obtain the health insurance price index for each industry.

To obtain the price index that is matched with the 1977 EEEC survey, the health insurance premium paid for each worker is regressed on the characteristics of the health insurance plan, a set of industry dummy variables, and a set of dummy variables that result from interacting region, urban/nonurban location, and white-collar/blue-collar occupation. Appendix table A3.2 displays the estimated coefficients of the industry dummy variables and the interaction terms. (The characteristics of the health insurance plan included in the equation are enumerated above. Because individual characteristics are controlled for explicitly in the fringe benefit demand equations estimated using the EEEC data, they are excluded from this hedonic health insurance price equation.)

The estimates of the industry dummy variables displayed in table A3.2 are qualitatively similar to those shown in table A3.1. This result

Table A3.2 **Hedonic Price Function for Health Insurance: Estimates Used with the 1977 EEEC Survey Data**

Independent Variable	Mean (Sample Proportion)	OLS Coefficient (Standard Error)
Industry: Agriculture	0.011	–43.13 (65.36)
Mining	0.017	226.71 (56.75)
Construction	0.036	79.69 (38.39)
Manufacturing	0.228	59.43 (19.92)
Transportation, Communication, Utilities	0.073	91.36 (28.51)
Sales	0.118	–22.29 (24.17)
Finance, Insurance, Real Estate	0.051	–25.97 (33.58)
Services (Repair)	0.043	–1.17 (35.13)
Services (Personal)	0.011	–48.36 (66.94)
Services (Entertainment)	0.007	–91.12 (84.04)
Services (Professional)	0.117	–13.06 (24.33)
Other or Unknown Industry	0.288	Omitted category
Region/Urban-Rural Location/Occupation:		
North/Urban/ White Collar	0.084	46.57 (52.30)
North Central/Urban/ White Collar	0.092	16.27 (51.87)
South/Urban/ White Collar	0.092	–58.04 (51.74)

Table A3.2 (*continued*)

Independent Variable	Mean (Sample Proportion)	OLS Coefficient (Standard Error)
West/Urban/ White Collar	0.063	1.17 (53.47)
North/Rural/ White Collar	0.013	-82.07 (74.53)
North Central/Rural/ White Collar	0.035	9.87 (58.96)
South/Rural/ White Collar	0.041	132.80 (58.18)
West/Rural/ White Collar	0.016	48.94 (69.19)
North/Urban/ Blue Collar	0.094	80.68 (51.83)
North Central/ Urban/Blue Collar	0.098	76.64 (51.33)
South/Urban/ Blue Collar	0.091	-67.96 (51.74)
West/Urban/ Blue Collar	0.069	71.93 (53.10)
North/Rural/ Blue Collar	0.017	-100.70 (69.53)
North Central/Rural/ Blue Collar	0.069	-78.01 (53.32)
South/Rural/ Blue Collar	0.102	-166.52 (51.70)
West/Rural/ Blue Collar	0.024	Omitted category
R-squared (adjusted)		0.305
F-ratio		41.215

NOTES: The equation estimated is an ordinary least squares regression of the primary insured's total annual group health insurance premium on the variables shown in the table, and a set of independent variables characterizing the health insurance package (see the text). The mean of the dependent variable (the annual health insurance premium) is $829.74 (with a standard deviation of $552.33). A sample of 4,764 individuals from the 1977–78 National Medical Care Expenditure Survey was used to estimate the equation.

suggests that the industry effects are robust to relatively minor changes in specification. The coefficients of the interaction terms suggest three findings. First, health insurance costs tend to be higher in urban than in rural areas (with the exception of white-collar workers in the South). Second, health insurance costs tend to be higher for blue-collar than for white-collar workers (with the rural South again providing the exception). Third, regional variations in health insurance are somewhat erratic and depend on occupation (white-collar or blue-collar) and urban-rural location. Indeed, it seems best to conclude that occupation and urban-rural location are considerably more important than region in determining health insurance costs.

The coefficients displayed in table A3.2 can be converted into a price index by a procedure similar to that outlined above for the industry price index. First, evaluate the health insurance premium at the mean of all the independent variables excluding the industry dummy variables and the region-location-occupation interaction terms. Call this *Prem″*. Take the sum of an industry coefficient and an interaction term coefficient. Since there are 10 industries that are of interest and 16 region-location-occupation groupings, there are a total of 160 such sums. Divide each sum by *Prem″* and add one to obtain the health insurance price index for each grouping. Each observation in the 1977 EEEC sample is assigned the appropriate price index value, based on its industry, region, urban-rural location, and whether the workers in the unit observed are white-collar or blue-collar.

NOTES

[1] It is tempting to apologize for the fact that the 1977 EEEC data are over a decade old, but they are the most recent firm-level data that are available for our purposes. The establishment-level data underlying the Employment Cost Index would be extremely useful, but they are unavailable. In using the 1977 EEEC data, we are forced to maintain the hypothesis that the economic relationships we estimate have not changed dramatically in the last 10 to 15 years.

[2] Note again that equations (2.5) and (2.36) define the inverse of (p_r/p_w) and (p_h/p_w), which are the relative prices used to estimate equations (2.34) and (2.35).

[3] We are grateful to Martin Murphy of the Bureau of Economic Analysis for allowing us access to the unpublished two-digit industry data from the National Income and Product Accounts (NIPA). Since the 1968–1982 data were obtained, the Bureau of Economic Analysis has discontinued

separating other labor income into pensions and group insurance at the two-digit industry level, even for internal (unpublished) use. Hence, the 1968–1982 series used here is the most up-to-date that can be obtained.

[4] Clearly, this is an undesirable assumption necessitated by the lack of available data similar to the National Medical Care Expenditure Survey for each year we examine. If the assumption is incorrect, we have an errors-in-variables problem. There is, however, no *a priori* reason to believe that interindustry relative costs of health insurance change dramatically over time.

[5] In calculating industry averages, we have used full-time equivalent employment in each industry, as reported in the NIPA. The NIPA also reports full-time and part-time employment in each industry. Using the latter as a measure of industry employment would give undue weight to part-time workers in industries that use part-timers heavily.

[6] Again, in calculating averages per employee, we have used the figures on full-time equivalent employees in each industry. Note that the measure of industry employment used matters to the computation of after-tax wages and salaries per employee because this is an imputation based on applying the industry average taxable income to the tax schedule. Total compensation is also affected by the use of full-time equivalent employment, because total compensation is the sum of after-tax wages and salaries, pension contributions, and health insurance contributions.

[7] The term "blue-collar worker" will be used throughout the discussion as synonymous with "production worker" or "nonoffice worker"; "white-collar worker" will be used as synonymous with "nonproduction worker" or "office worker." Different data sets use different terminology for the same concept, and it seems best to choose standard terminology.

[8] The use of interpolation and extrapolation for median age by industry and year may result in measurement error and its attendant problems. In this case, the only alternative would be to omit the variable.

[9] Note that the minimum capital-labor ratio displayed in table 3.1 is zero. This occurs because in 1968 and 1969, the legal services industry had no capital consumption allowance.

[10] We believe it would be useful to use an industry-specific estimate of job tenure as a proxy for specific human capital in future work. Unfortunately, although the data to obtain such estimates exist, no one has yet derived the estimates.

[11] We have not attempted to include any variable indicating the degree to which compensation is determined by collective bargaining in the present analysis (although we do so in the analysis that uses the EEEC data). The NIPA data do not report any measure of unionization by industry, and although it might be possible to construct such a variable from the Current Population Survey (or some other source) and match it to the NIPA data, we are willing to view unionization as an industry-specific effect that is captured by the industry dummies included in this model.

[12] We assume that an increase in the share of total compensation paid as pensions or health insurance implies greater total expenditure on pensions or health insurance. So long as total compensation is growing, this assumption is correct.

[13] The 1976 EEEC survey was alone among the EEEC surveys in being limited to establishments with at least 20 employees.

[14] The EEEC survey refers to workers as either office or nonoffice workers. In keeping with our standard terminology, these groups will be referred to as white-collar or blue-collar.

[15] It is worth noting that the results on unionism reported here are in accord with time-series estimates of the impact of unions on the mix of total compensation (Long and Scott 1982; Alpert 1987).

[16] It could be argued that the skill proxy is in fact an endogenous variable – that workers who are

provided more fringe benefits will accumulate longer tenure and greater firm-specific human capital. It turns out, however, that the other coefficients estimated in the model are robust to the exclusion of the skill proxy variable.

[17] Industries showing consistently high shares of pension benefits, other things equal, include: anthracite mining and oil and gas extraction; petroleum and coal manufacturing; a relatively small part of the transportation sector (local transit, water transport, and pipelines); and motion pictures. Four manufacturing industries (food, paper, printing and publishing, and instruments) show especially low shares of pension benefits, as do security services, and health and educational services.

In addition to having high shares of pension compensation, anthracite mining and motion pictures also have unusually high shares of health insurance. Six manufacturing industries have unusually *low* shares of health insurance: food, tobacco, printing and publishing, chemicals, petroleum and coal, and instruments. A significant part of the transportation and utilities sector (trucking and warehousing, air transport, communication, and electricity and gas) provide low shares of health insurance, other things equal. The same is true of much of the financial sector (banking, credit agencies, security services, and insurance carriers) and of business, health, and educational services.

We find two points interesting in these industry results. First, there is much diversity of fringe benefit provision within each major (one-digit) industry grouping. This suggests that, if possible, it is useful to control for industry at the two-digit level. Second, other things equal, an industry that tends to offer a high share of compensation as pensions tends also to offer a high share of compensation as health insurance.

[18] "Generous" hospital benefits are defined as 365 days or more of basic hospital benefits, or, for those with no basic hospital benefits, $250,000 of major medical coverage.

4

Simulation of Alternative Policies

The empirical work developed in chapter 3 yielded a variety of information about the demand for fringe benefits and the existence of tradeoffs among different components of compensation. Three main findings about the effects of income and tax-prices on the demand for fringe benefits emerged. First, the demand for wage benefits is income inelastic, whereas the demand for pensions and health insurance is income elastic. Second, both pensions and health insurance are good substitutes for wage benefits, and pensions appear to be a better substitute for wages than is health insurance. And third, pensions and health insurance may be complements, but the evidence on this point is not strong. (In a strictly statistical sense, one would have to conclude that the elasticity of substitution between pensions and health insurance is zero. There is nevertheless a strong hint of complementarity between pensions and health insurance.) The price, income, and substitution elasticities that underlie these three summary statements constitute our basic findings.

In this chapter, the elasticities derived in chapter 3 are used to gain an understanding of how various tax policy changes would influence the demand for, and provision of, fringe benefits. In many ways, the simulations presented in this chapter are the real payoff to the chapter 3 empirical work.

We present simulations of three alternative policies. First, we investigate the impact of the 1986 Tax Reform Act on the provision of fringe benefits. Second, we simulate the effects of taxing health insurance contributions as income. Finally, we examine how taxing employer contributions to both pensions and health insurance would affect the provision of fringe benefits.

97

The latter two simulated policies involve a basic change in the tax base, that is, taxation of one or more components of compensation that are presently untaxed. Indeed, one of the main reasons for broadening the tax base by taxing employer contributions to pensions and health insurance is to raise federal revenues and forestall further erosion of the tax base. Hence, it is important to simulate the effects of the changes in tax policy on federal revenues. As will become clear below, estimated revenue effects can be computed in a straightforward way in the course of the simulation. Accordingly, this chapter also presents estimates of the effects of each simulated policy on federal revenues.

Simulation Strategy

Simulating Compensation Shares

The simulation strategy can be outlined in two steps. First, suppose that one of the four models estimated using the National Income and Product Accounts (NIPA) data in the last chapter represents the mechanism by which fringe benefit shares are determined in the U.S. economy. Using a superscript ^ (hat) to denote estimated coefficients and predicted values of compensation shares, any one of these estimated models may be written:

$$\hat{s}_r = \hat{a}_r + \hat{b}_{rr}[ln(p_r/p_w)] + \hat{b}_{rh}[ln(p_h/p_w)] + \hat{b}_r[ln(m/P^*)] + \hat{d}_{r1}[x_1] + \ldots + \hat{d}_{rK}[x_K] \tag{4.1}$$

$$\hat{s}_h = \hat{a}_h + \hat{b}_{rh}[ln(p_r/p_w)] + \hat{b}_{hh}[ln(p_h/p_w)] + \hat{b}_h[ln(m/P^*)] + \hat{d}_{h1}[x_1] + \ldots + \hat{d}_{hK}[x_K]. \tag{4.2}$$

Equations (4.1) and (4.2) show the predicted (or estimated or forecast) shares of pensions and health insurance ($\hat{s}_r$ and $\hat{s}_h$) as a function of relative prices [(p_r/p_w) and (p_h/p_w)], real total compensation (m/P^*), and other characteristics, such as age and gender ($x_1, \ldots, x_K$). The $\hat{a}_i$, $\hat{b}_{ij}$, $\hat{b}_i$, and $\hat{d}_{ik}$ are estimated parameter values.

Second, in order to simulate the effect of any alternative tax system on fringe benefit provision, we use an algorithm to simulate the relative prices $[(p_r/p_w)$ and $(p_h/p_w)]$ and income (m/P^*) implied by that alternative tax system. Each of these algorithms is similar to the algorithm that imputed marginal taxes and after-tax income in the last chapter. Denoting these new simulated relative prices and income by a superscript ˜ (tilde), equations (4.1) and (4.2) may be rewritten:

$$\tilde{s}_r = \hat{a}_r + \hat{b}_{rr}[ln(\widetilde{p_r/p_w})] + \hat{b}_{rh}[ln(\widetilde{p_h/p_w})] + \qquad (4.3)$$
$$\hat{b}_r[ln(\widetilde{m/P^*})] + \hat{d}_{r1}[x_1] + \ldots + \hat{d}_{rK}[x_K]$$

$$\tilde{s}_h = \hat{a}_h + \hat{b}_{rh}[ln(\widetilde{p_r/p_w})] + \hat{b}_{hh}[ln(\widetilde{p_h/p_w})] + \qquad (4.4)$$
$$\hat{b}_h[ln(\widetilde{m/P^*})] + \hat{d}_{h1}[x_1] + \ldots + \hat{d}_{hK}[x_K].$$

Substituting the simulated relative prices $[(\widetilde{p_r/p_w})$ and $(\widetilde{p_h/p_w})]$ and income $[(\widetilde{m/P^*})]$ into equations (4.3) and (4.4) results in a set of simulated shares of pension benefits and health insurance benefits under the new tax system. These simulated compensation shares are denoted by $\tilde{s}_r$ and $\tilde{s}_h$. (The simulated share of wages, $\tilde{s}_w$, is obtained as a residual, since $\tilde{s}_w + \tilde{s}_r + \tilde{s}_h = 1$.) A main goal of this chapter is to obtain these simulated compensation shares and to compare them with predicted and other simulated compensation shares.

The simulation strategy just outlined is a single-step approach. In fact, the simulations presented in this chapter are augmented by a second step. This is because the compensation shares used to construct P^* in the simulated real total compensation term $[ln(\widetilde{m/P^*})]$ of equations (4.3) and (4.4) are actual (that is, historically observed) shares, rather than the shares that the single-step simulation suggests would occur under the alternative tax policy. [Recall from equation (2.20) that P^* is a share-weighted sum of logarithmic prices.] Recomputing P^* using the new simulated compensation shares, and resimulating equations (4.3) and (4.4), yields second-step simulated compensation shares that frequently differ substantially from the single-step simulated shares. It is possible, of course, to iterate this procedure, recomputing P^* after the second step using the second-step simulated shares, and again resimulating the model. However, experimentation has shown that the differences between the second- and third-step simulated shares are minimal, and certainly not worth the added computational expense.

Note that the simulation strategy assumes that simulated changes in marginal tax rates and the tax treatment of employer contributions have no effect on (a) before-tax total compensation, (b) the demographic and other control variables (x_1 through x_K) included in the estimated equations, or (c) the structure of demand for compensation—that is, that the parameter estimates ($\hat{a}_i$, $\hat{b}_{ij}$, $\hat{b}_i$, and $\hat{d}_{ik}$) of the model used in the simulation.

Simulating Real Expenditures on Compensation

The simulation strategy outlined above yields simulated *shares* of wages, pensions, and health insurance. It is useful for some purposes to convert these shares into *real expenditures* on wages, pensions, and health insurance. Knowing about real expenditures on compensation—that is, the *quantities* of various forms of compensation that workers receive—is useful for three reasons. First, real or constant-dollar expenditures on compensation have been a perennial concern of employers. Second, from the point of view of policy, it is more important to know how changes in the tax treatment of fringe benefits would alter real benefits received by workers than to know whether the compensation package shifted toward or away from a given component of compensation.

Third, consumer theory offers no prediction about what will happen to the *share* of total compensation received in form i in response to a change in tax treatment.[1] For example, taxing health insurance contributions (that is, raising the price of health insurance) could either increase or decrease the share of compensation received as health insurance depending on the elasticity of demand for health insurance. But consumer theory implies that the compensated demand curve for health insurance must be downward-sloping, and that taxing health insurance should lead to reduced quantities of health insurance demanded (holding constant real purchasing power and all other demand-determining factors). In general, it is simpler to interpret simulations that are stated in terms of changes in compensation quantities (that is, real expenditures) than in terms of compensation shares. Retrieving simulated real expenditures on each form of compensation from our estimates is straightforward. By definition, the share of compensation received in form i is:

$$s_i = p_i z_i / m. \qquad (4.5)$$

It follows that simulated real expenditures on compensation received in form i ($\tilde{z}_i$) can be obtained by substituting the simulated s_i, m, and p_i into identity (4.5) and solving for $\tilde{z}_i$:

$$\tilde{z}_i = \tilde{s}_i \tilde{m} / \tilde{p}_i. \qquad (4.6)$$

Simulated Comparisons

Two kinds of simulated comparison prove useful and are presented below. First, we ask how a different tax treatment of fringe benefits would have altered fringe benefit provision during the past 20 years. That is, how would fringe benefit provision have differed if fringe benefits had been treated differently under the tax system that existed in each year from 1969 through 1982? These simulations are referred to as simulations *under the tax systems existing in 1969–1982*.

Second, from the point of view of current policy, it is important to understand how changes in the tax treatment of fringe benefits could be expected to alter fringe benefit provision under the current tax system — that is, the system initiated under the Tax Reform Act of 1986. These simulations are referred to as simulations *under the 1986 tax reform*.

These two simulated comparisons are discussed further presently.

1. *Simulations Under Tax Systems Existing in 1969–1982*. Simulating the effects of changes in the tax treatment of fringe benefits under the tax systems that existed in each year from 1969 through 1982 is accomplished in two steps. First, the shares of wages, pensions, and health insurance *predicted* under the tax system in effect in each year are obtained from equations (4.1) and (4.2). These shares provide the basis — or "counterfactual" — for the simulated comparisons. Second, the simulated shares under the same tax system, but with an altered tax

treatment of fringe benefits superimposed, are obtained by the method described above [see equations (4.3) and (4.4)].

The result is a comparison of simulated shares with *predicted* shares. Comparing the simulated shares with *actually observed* shares would be inappropriate because the actual shares incorporate a random error that the simulations cannot incorporate. To see why, examine equations (4.1) through (4.4). These suggest that a comparison of predicted with simulated shares should be a clean comparison: the predicted shares indicate what the model predicts compensation shares would be under a set of actually observed conditions, whereas the simulated shares indicate what the model predicts compensation shares would be under some hypothetical conditions. If instead of using the predicted shares as the "counterfactual" to the simulated shares, we used the actual shares, we would contaminate the comparison with random errors for which the simulation, by definition, does not control. Accordingly, the tables in this chapter that report simulations under the tax systems existing in 1969–1982 compare *simulated* with *predicted* shares (or real expenditures), in order to present a clean picture of how a different tax treatment of fringe benefits would have altered compensation in 1969 through 1982.

2. Simulations Under the 1986 Tax Reform. Simulating the effects of changes in the tax treatment of fringe benefits under the 1986 tax reform is also accomplished in two steps. First, we simulate the shares of wages, pensions, and health insurance that would have been observed in each year from 1969 through 1982 if the 1986 tax system had been in effect. These shares provide the counterfactual for the 1986 tax reform simulation. Second, we simulate the shares that would have been observed in each year if an altered tax treatment of fringe benefits had been superimposed on the basic 1986 tax system. [In both of these steps, we use the method developed earlier and summarized by equations (4.3) and (4.4).]

The result is a comparison between two simulated shares – one under the 1986 tax reform, the other under the 1986 tax reform with a changed tax treatment of fringe benefits. The comparison is a clean one, in that in that there is no random error in either of the simulated shares used in the comparison.

Revenue Effects

The effects of each simulated tax policy on federal revenues can be appraised by an extension of the two-step simulation procedure. The strategy here is to simulate, for each observation, a new level of before-tax wages that accounts for the fact that the mix of wages and fringe benefits may change as a result of the simulated tax law. Once computed, this new level of before-tax wages is applied to the tax law being simulated in order to obtain (again for each observation) a simulated tax bill under the new law. If the simulated law taxes one or more kinds of fringe benefits in addition to wages, then the dollar expenditure on taxable fringe benefits is added to the new level of before-tax wages before computing the tax bill.

The new simulated level of before-tax wages, which we will call $(\widetilde{z_w p_w})$, is computed by subtracting from the observed before-tax total compensation (TC_b) the simulated expenditure on fringe benefits. (TC_b is simply the sum of observed before-tax wages and expenditures on fringe benefits.) Simulated expenditures on fringe benefits are computed by multiplying simulated after-tax total compensation (TC_a, which is the sum of simulated after-tax earnings and observed fringe benefits) by the simulated share of after-tax compensation allocated to fringe benefits ($\tilde{s}_r + \tilde{s}_h$). (The simulated fringe benefit shares must be multiplied by after-tax compensation because the simulated benefit shares predict the proportion of after-tax total compensation that will be allocated to fringe benefits.)

Accordingly, the new simulated level of before-tax wages is:

$$(\widetilde{z_w p_w}) = TC_b - [TC_a(\tilde{s}_r + \tilde{s}_h)]. \tag{4.7}$$

This is the dollar amount that, either by itself or with taxable fringe benefits added to it, is applied to whichever tax schedule is being simulated in order to compute the tax bill of each observation in the sample. We compute the aggregate tax bill by summing the taxes paid by each observation in the sample.

Distributional Effects

Finally, it is important to understand whether changing the tax treatment of fringe benefits would have uneven effects on different groups of workers depending on their income. To gain some insight into the distributional effects of changing the tax treatment of fringe benefits, we offer summaries of effects for three groups of industries—those in which average earnings were between $11,630 and $17,041, those in which average earnings were between $17,643 and $22,550, and those in which average earnings were between $23,103 and $39,498, all in 1982 current dollars.

The unit of observation we are using for our simulations is the industry, which is not an ideal unit of observation for a distributional analysis. Clearly, the individual or the household would be preferable. Nevertheless, an understanding of how changing the tax treatment of fringe benefits would have a differential impact on industries in which average earnings differ should provide some notion of how taxing fringe benefits would affect households in different income categories.

Further Issues

A variety of further issues must be handled in implementing the simulations. Three of these deserve general mention here because they apply to all of the simulations discussed. Specifics of these issues will be raised below in discussing the simulations.

1. *Selection of Estimates Used in Simulations*. Recall that chapter 3 reported estimates using two different data sets, a variety of methods of imputing the marginal tax rates (and hence relative prices) facing a group of workers, and both weighted and unweighted joint generalized least squares. Clearly, any of the sets of parameter values estimated in the last chapter could serve as a basis for simulation.

With one modification noted in the next subsection, the simulations presented below are based on estimates from the NIPA data, using the *joint-filing* tax scheme and *weighted* joint generalized least squares (WJGLS). These estimates appear in chapter 3, tables 3.2 and 3.3. We have used these estimates because they are arguably the most representative of the entire private U.S. economy (both because they are weighted by total compensation and because they use the NIPA data). Hence, the simulations can be directly interpreted as representing policy impacts on the private U.S. economy.

In order to ensure that the results of our simulations are not peculiar to our choice of underlying estimates, we have computed a variety of alternative simulations. We have used estimates from both the NIPA and Employer Expenditure for Employee Compensation (EEEC) data sets, based on different imputations of marginal tax rates, and based on weighted and unweighted estimation procedures. It turns out that variation among these alternative simulations is minor, which is not surprising given the congruence of the various estimates reported in chapter 3. Hence, we report only the simulations based on the NIPA estimates using joint-filing and WJGLS.

2. Model Restrictions. We have modified the estimates of the joint-filing, WJGLS model in one way. Rather than allow the elasticity of substitution between pensions and health insurance (σ_{rh}) to take its estimated value of -3.24 (see the row labeled σ_{rh} in table 3.3), we restrict σ_{rh} to -1.0 in all simulations. This restriction is imposed because the standard error of σ_{rh} is so high that (statistically) σ_{rh} itself cannot be distinguished from zero. Although it could be argued that σ_{rh} should be restricted to zero, it seems reasonable to allow some degree of complementarity between pensions and health insurance, in view of the large negative point estimates of σ_{rh}. Hence we compromise by setting σ_{rh} equal to one. We have checked the degree to which this restriction affects the simulations and found the effects to be surprisingly minor.

3. Decomposition of Simulated Effects. Understanding of the simulations is aided by decomposing the simulated effects of any change in tax regime into three parts. Recall that the simulated shares of pensions and health insurance are computed as:

$$\tilde{s}_r = \hat{a}_r + \hat{b}_{rr}[ln(\widetilde{p_r/p_w})] + \hat{b}_{rh}[ln(\widetilde{p_h/p_w})] + \qquad (4.3)$$
$$\hat{b}_r[ln(\widetilde{m/P^*})] + \hat{d}_{r1}[x_1] + \ldots + \hat{d}_{rK}[x_K]$$

$$\tilde{s}_h = \hat{a}_h + \hat{b}_{rh}[ln(\widetilde{p_r/p_w})] + \hat{b}_{hh}[ln(\widetilde{p_h/p_w})] + \qquad (4.4)$$
$$\hat{b}_h[ln(\widetilde{m/P^*})] + \hat{d}_{h1}[x_1] + \ldots + \hat{d}_{hK}[x_K],$$

where $\tilde{s}_r$ and $\tilde{s}_h$ denote simulated compensation shares, $(\widetilde{p_r/p_w})$ and $(\widetilde{p_h/p_w})$ denote simulated relative prices, and $(\widetilde{m/P^*})$ denotes simulated real income. In simulations under the tax systems existing in 1969–1982, these simulated shares are compared with the compensation shares predicted for 1969–1982 ($\hat{s}_r$ and $\hat{s}_h$), which are computed from equations (4.1) and (4.2). In our simulations under the 1986 tax reform, these simulated shares are compared with another set of simulated shares—the shares that our model tells us would prevail if fringe benefits remained untaxed under the 1986 tax reform.

The difference between each simulated share and each predicted (or other simulated) share can be decomposed into the following three parts:

(a) the change in compensation share that results from changing only the relative price terms $[(\widetilde{p_r/p_w})$ and $(\widetilde{p_h/p_w})]$ in equations (4.3) and (4.4), but holding real compensation and all other terms constant;

(b) the change that results from changing the price index (P^*) of the real income term $(\widetilde{m/P^*})$, but holding constant money income (m) and all other terms in equations (4.3) and (4.4); and

(c) the change that results from changing money income (m) in the real income term $(\widetilde{m/P^*})$, but holding constant all other terms in equations (4.3) and (4.4).

The first of these three effects can be recognized as a pure substitution (or price) effect, the second as an ordinary income effect, and the third and an additional income effect that we will call the "extra" income effect. This "extra" income effect is unconventional, but it may occur if a change in the tax system, in addition to altering relative prices, also alters the level of total compensation available to workers. The existence of the extra income effect will be discussed further in the context of each simulation.[2]

Impact of the 1986 Tax Reform

The 1986 Tax Reform

Primarily because it lowered marginal tax rates under the federal individual income tax, the Tax Reform Act of 1986 has potentially important implications for the provision of fringe benefits by employers. Several existing studies bear out the hypothesis that rising marginal tax rates on wages during the 1960s and 1970s led to increases in the fringe benefit share of compensation, and it follows that lowering the tax-price of wages should have the opposite effect. Such a hypothesis could be based loosely on a theory like that outlined in chapter 2: since lower marginal tax rates on wages reduce the tax-price of wages relative to fringe benefits, it stands to reason that the quantity of wage compensation will increase, and the quantity of fringe benefit compensation will decrease, as a result of tax reform. That is, the reduced tax rates on earnings should result in substitution of wages for fringe benefits.[3]

Although the substitution or tax-price effect is the most obvious avenue by which the 1986 reform could be expected to affect the mix of compensation, income effects are also possible. Indeed, two separate income effects, both of which would tend to offset the pure substitution of tax reform, may arise (see above). The first is the ordinary income effect that arises because price changes lead to changes in real purchasing power. The second income effect may arise because the 1986 tax reform increased the proportion of total federal revenues raised by the corporation income tax, lowering the burden placed directly on households through the individual income tax. If corporations bear the full burden of increases in the corporation income tax, it is possible that the household sector will experience an increase (or at least a perceived increase) in disposable income as a result of the 1986 reform. If so, then the reform would have an additional income effect—

or what we called the "extra" income effect above—on the demand for fringe benefits. Both of these income effects would tend to offset the substitution effect of the reform; the empirical findings of chapter 3 suggest that lowered marginal tax rates will tend to dampen the demand for fringe benefits, but that increased incomes will tend to strengthen that demand.

Whether the extra income effect actually occurs is an awkward question, depending as it does on who bears the burden of the corporation income tax. The controversy over who bears the corporation income tax is as profound as any in economics—see Pechman (1987, pp. 141–145) for a sampling of conclusions about the incidence of the tax. It is not at all clear whether corporations bear the full burden, part of the burden, or none of the burden of the corporation income tax. But an assumption about the burden of the corporation income tax is in effect an assumption about whether the 1986 Tax Reform Act has raised households' nominal disposable incomes. Given the controversy surrounding the burden of the corporation income tax, it seems important to examine the simulated effects of the 1986 tax reform under alternative assumptions about whether households experience increased incomes as a result of the reform, and we provide such an examination below.

The 1986 tax reform is simulated by the procedure outlined above. First, an algorithm is constructed that creates the relative prices $(\widetilde{p_r/p_w})$ and $(\widetilde{p_h/p_w})$ and income $(\widetilde{m/P^*})$ that would have prevailed in each industry and each year from 1969 through 1982 if the 1986 tax reform legislation had existed in those years. Since we are relying on the estimates from the joint-filing tax scheme, relative prices are simulated by applying taxable income, computed as annual gross earnings minus three exemptions and the joint-filing standard deduction, to the 1988 joint-filing tax table. (The 1988 tax system is used to simulate the tax reform because 1988 was the first year the system was fully in effect.) It is necessary to deflate the complete tax system—exemptions, standard deduction, and tax brackets—to a level appropriate to the year in question. We do so using the Consumer Price Index.

The simulated relative prices and income are then substituted into equations (4.3) and (4.4) to obtain the simulated shares of pensions and health insurance benefits ($\bar{s}_r$ and $\bar{s}_h$). Note again that the demographic and other control variables (x_1 through x_K), which also influence the mix of compensation, are held constant in the simulation because they are assumed unaffected by tax reform.

In summary, simulations based on the chapter 3 estimates of preferences for wages and nonwages are needed in order to answer questions about the effects of the 1986 tax reform on the provision of fringe benefits. Questions about the 1986 tax reform to be addressed in the remainder of this section include the following: How would we expect tax reform to affect the shares of wages, pensions, and health insurance in total compensation, and how would we expect tax reform to affect real expenditures on each component? To what degree is tax reform responsible for substitution of wages for fringe benefits? Have pensions and health insurance benefits been differently affected by the reform? Have the fringe benefits of different groups of workers been differently affected? What are the effects of the reform on tax revenues?

Simulated Effects of the 1986 Tax Reform

Table 4.1 shows how the tax system enacted by the 1986 tax reform would have altered real expenditures on compensation, and compensation shares, if it had been in effect during 1969 through 1982. All effects are in percentage terms and averaged over the 1969–1982 period. The first panel shows the *total effects* of the 1986 tax reform—that is, the sum of the substitution, ordinary income, and extra income effects. The second panel isolates the *substitution effects*. The third panel *disaggregates the total effects on real expenditures* into effects on low-wage, medium-wage, and high-wage industries.

Consider the following pair of entries in table 4.1. The first entry in the first panel (9.4) indicates that real wage expenditures (or the quantity of wages) would have been 9.4 percent greater on average during 1969–1982 if the 1986 tax reform system had been in effect in those years. The first entry in the second panel (1.6) indicates that the lower marginal tax rates (lower tax-price of wages) implied by the 1986 reform would by themselves have increased real wage expenditures by just 1.6 percent. It

Table 4.1   Simulated Effects of the 1986 Tax Reform: Average Percentage Changes Under Tax Systems Existing 1969–1982

	Wages	Pensions	Health Insurance
Total Effects of 1986 Tax Reform on:			
Real Expenditures	9.4	0.9	10.4
Compensation Shares	–0.3	–1.4	7.7
Substitution Effects of 1986 Tax Reform on:			
Real Expenditures	1.6	–18.5	–6.1
Compensation Shares	0.7	–13.1	0.7
Total Effects on Real Expenditures, by Industry Group:			
Aggregate	9.4	0.9	10.4
Low-Wage Industries	5.0	1.9	8.2
Medium-Wage Industries	8.9	0.5	11.3
High-Wage Industries	13.5	0.7	10.4

NOTES: The figures show how replacing the tax systems in effect during 1969 through 1982 with the tax system implied by the 1986 tax reform would have changed real expenditures on compensation and shares of compensation. Changes are shown in annual percentage terms, averaged over the 14 years. "Total effect" refers to the sum of the substitution, ordinary income, and extra income effects. The substitution effect isolates the impact of the changing tax-price of wages relative to pensions and health insurance.

follows that most of the simulated *total* increase of 9.4 percent is the result of the income effects of tax reform, rather than lower marginal tax rates. If the 1986 tax reform implied a tax system that lowered marginal tax rates without changing households' real purchasing power, the simulated increase in real expenditures on wages would be only 1.6 percent. Other entries in table 4.1 may be interpreted and compared similarly.

1. *Aggregate Effects.* The results shown in table 4.1 suggest that, overall during 1969–1982, the tax system represented by the 1986 reforms would have increased *real expenditures* on wages and health insurance received by workers, and would have had little effect on real expenditures on pensions. These are the total effects of the tax reform, which assume that tax reform has the capacity to change real purchasing power (see the "Graphical Treatment of the Decomposition" below). The

increase in real expenditures on health insurance is driven by the large income effect of tax reform, whereas the increase in real expenditures on wages results from both income and substitution effects.

One could also consider the effects of the 1986 tax reform absent any income effects (see the substitution effects in the second panel of table 4.1). But it seems implausible that the tax reform included some automatic mechanism for holding purchasing power constant; hence, the total effects in the top panel are the preferred simulations of the 1986 tax reform.

Regarding compensation *shares*, the simulations suggest that the mix of compensation would have shifted toward health insurance and away from pensions, with little effect on the wage share. Keep in mind that consumer theory offers no prediction about the direction of changes in shares, since these latter changes are determined by changes in both relative prices and quantities. Again, the increase in the health insurance share in this simulation appears to be driven mainly by the income effects of tax reform, which lead to a large increase in health insurance quantities.

2. Distributional Effects. The bottom panel of table 4.1 divides the total effects of the tax reform on *real expenditures* into effects on different groups of workers. The simulations suggest that workers in high-wage industries experience much larger increases in real expenditures on wages than do workers in low-wage industries. This difference results because most of the increase in wage expenditures is driven by the income effects of the tax reform, with workers in high-wage industries experiencing greater income effects than others.

The 1986 tax reform appears to have relatively even distributional effects on pension and health insurance expenditures. Workers in low-wage industries have a somewhat larger increase in demand for pensions, and only slightly lower increase in demand for health insurance, than do workers in medium- and high-wage industries.

3. Decomposing the Simulated Effects. Further insight into the results displayed in table 4.1 can be obtained by decomposing the effects

Table 4.2 Simulated Effects of the 1986 Tax Reform on Real Wage Expenditures, 1969–1982

(a) Year	(b) Predicted	(c) Simulated: Only Relative Prices Changed	(d) Simulated: Relative Prices and P^* Changed	(e) Simulated: Relative Prices, P^*, and m Changed	(f) Substitution Effect (Percent)	(g) Ordinary Income Effect (Percent)	(h) Extra Income Effect (Percent)	(i) Total Effect (Percent)
1969	12045	12192	12913	13438	1.22	5.99	4.36	11.56
1970	12313	12427	12929	13283	0.93	4.08	2.88	7.88
1971	12976	13080	13558	13861	0.80	3.68	2.34	6.82
1972	13320	13435	13917	14134	0.86	3.62	1.63	6.11
1973	13118	13248	13764	14030	0.99	3.93	2.03	6.95
1974	12729	12882	13479	13818	1.20	4.69	2.66	8.56
1975	13025	13191	13796	13991	1.27	4.64	1.50	7.42
1976	13297	13480	14118	14264	1.38	4.80	1.10	7.27
1977	13533	13726	14333	14381	1.43	4.49	0.35	6.27
1978	13266	13493	14257	14402	1.71	5.76	1.09	8.56
1979	13149	13357	14083	14311	1.58	5.52	1.73	8.84
1980	12838	13079	13909	14271	1.88	6.47	2.82	11.16
1981	12409	12721	13751	14241	2.51	8.30	3.95	14.76
1982	12854	13116	13972	14374	2.04	6.66	3.13	11.83
Mean	12936	13141	13861	14154	1.58	5.57	2.26	9.42

NOTES: Columns (b) through (e) show real wage expenditures by year (these may also be thought of as quantities or constant dollar expenditures). The predicted figures (column (b)) provide the base for our comparisons, showing wage expenditures predicted by our model under prices and income that existed in each year. Column (c) shows wage expenditures if only the substitution effect occurred, column (d) shows wage expenditures if both substitution and ordinary income effects occurred, and column (e) shows wage expenditures if substitution, ordinary income, and extra income effects occurred.

Columns (f) through (i) show substitution, ordinary income, extra income, and total effects in percentage terms, and are computed from the figures in columns (b) through (e).

of the 1986 tax reform into substitution and income effects. Table 4.2 shows the results of decomposing the effect of tax reform on real wage expenditures (or quantities), and tables 4.3 and 4.4 show the decompositions for pensions and health insurance.

Columns (b) and (e) of tables 4.2, 4.3, and 4.4 give the information needed to compute the total effect of the 1986 tax reform. The columns labeled "Predicted" (b) show the real expenditures on wages, pensions, and health insurance predicted by the model for each year from 1969 through 1982, given the relative prices and income that actually existed. This is the counterfactual—that is, the base against which all the simulated changes are to be compared. The columns labeled "Simulated: Relative Prices, P^*, and m Changed" (e) show the real expenditures that would have prevailed in each year if the 1986 tax reform had been in effect. Hence, the difference between columns (b) and (e) is the total effect of the tax reform.

Columns (b) and (c) give the information needed to compute the substitution effect. The columns labeled "Simulated: Only Relative Prices Changed" (c) show the simulated effect of changing relative prices but holding all else constant. Hence, the difference between columns (b) and (c) is the substitution effect of the tax reform.

The ordinary income effect is obtained from columns (c) and (d). The columns labeled "Simulated: Relative Prices and P^* Changed" (d) show the simulated effect of changing relative prices *and* the price index (P^*) in the denominator of the real income term, but holding all else constant. Hence, the difference between columns (c) and (d) is the ordinary income effect. Finally, since column (e) shows the total simulated effect [that is, the effect of changing relative prices, the price index (P^*), and the money income term (m)], the difference between columns (d) and (e) is the extra income effect.

The remaining columns of tables 4.2, 4.3, and 4.4 show the various effects of tax reform in percentage terms. Specifically, the substitution effect in column (f) is calculated by dividing the difference between columns (b) and (c) by column (b). Similarly, the ordinary income effect in column (g) is calculated by dividing the difference between columns (d) and (c) by column (b). The extra income effect in column (h) is

Table 4.3 Simulated Effects of the 1986 Tax Reform on Real Pension Expenditures, 1969–1982

(a) Year	(b) Predicted	(c) Simulated: Only Relative Prices Changed	(d) Simulated: Relative Prices and P^* Changed	(e) Simulated: Relative Prices, P^*, and m Changed	(f) Substitution Effect (Percent)	(g) Ordinary Income Effect (Percent)	(h) Extra Income Effect (Percent)	(i) Total Effect (Percent)
1969	582	438	544	623	−24.74	18.21	13.57	7.04
1970	607	501	579	633	−17.46	12.85	8.90	4.28
1971	747	642	721	770	−14.06	10.58	6.56	3.08
1972	831	717	803	840	−13.72	10.35	4.45	1.08
1973	831	710	801	846	−14.56	10.95	5.42	1.81
1974	829	687	792	849	−17.13	12.67	6.88	2.41
1975	956	804	917	952	−15.90	11.82	3.66	−0.42
1976	1068	901	1026	1053	−15.64	11.70	2.53	−1.40
1977	1113	942	1070	1083	−15.36	11.50	1.17	−2.70
1978	1141	933	1089	1120	−18.23	13.67	2.72	−1.84
1979	1126	926	1077	1124	−17.76	13.41	4.17	−0.18
1980	1122	894	1065	1138	−20.32	15.24	6.51	1.43
1981	1144	858	1070	1170	−25.00	18.53	8.74	2.27
1982	1237	997	1175	1262	−19.40	14.39	7.03	2.02
Mean	1024	835	977	1033	−18.46	13.87	5.47	0.88

NOTES: Columns (b) through (e) show real pension expenditures by year (these may also be thought of as quantities or constant dollar expenditures). The predicted figures (column (b)) provide the base for our comparisons, showing pension expenditures predicted by our model under prices and income that existed in each year. Column (c) shows pension expenditures if only the substitution effect occurred, column (d) shows pension expenditures if both substitution and ordinary income effects occurred, and column (e) shows pension expenditures if substitution, ordinary income, and extra income effects occurred.

Columns (f) through (i) show substitution, ordinary income, extra income, and total effects in percentage terms, and are computed from the figures in columns (b) through (e).

Table 4.4 Simulated Effects of the 1986 Tax Reform on Real Health Insurance Expenditures, 1969–1982

(a)	(b)	(c)	(d)	(e)	(f)	(g)	(h)	(i)
Year	Predicted	Simulated: Only Relative Prices Changed	Simulated: Relative Prices and P^* Changed	Simulated: Relative Prices, P^*, and m Changed	Substitution Effect (Percent)	Ordinary Income Effect (Percent)	Extra Income Effect (Percent)	Total Effect (Percent)
1969	466	441	508	557	-5.36	14.38	10.52	19.53
1970	542	521	573	609	-3.87	9.59	6.64	12.36
1971	596	574	624	656	-3.69	8.39	5.37	10.07
1972	581	560	607	627	-3.61	8.09	3.44	7.92
1973	609	586	638	665	-3.78	8.54	4.43	9.20
1974	729	695	768	808	-4.66	10.01	5.49	10.84
1975	911	867	957	985	-4.83	9.88	3.07	8.12
1976	982	933	1033	1055	-4.99	10.18	2.24	7.43
1977	885	841	925	933	-4.97	9.49	0.90	5.42
1978	951	893	1006	1028	-6.10	11.88	2.31	8.10
1979	1059	995	1115	1153	-6.04	11.33	3.59	8.88
1980	1074	1000	1140	1199	-6.89	13.04	5.49	11.64
1981	1026	939	1106	1185	-8.48	16.28	7.70	15.50
1982	1039	967	1100	1162	-6.93	12.80	5.97	11.84
Mean	892	838	944	985	-6.05	11.88	4.60	10.43

NOTES: Columns (b) through (e) show real health insurance expenditures by year (these may also be thought of as quantities or constant dollar expenditures). The predicted figures (column (b)) provide the base for our comparisons, showing health insurance expenditures predicted by our model under prices and income that existed in each year. Column (c) shows health insurance expenditures if only the substitution effect occurred, column (d) shows health insurance expenditures if both substitution and ordinary income effects occurred, and column (e) shows health insurance expenditures if substitution, ordinary income, and extra income effects occurred.

Columns (f) through (i) show substitution, ordinary income, extra income, and total effects in percentage terms, and are computed from the figures in columns (b) through (e).

computed by dividing the difference between columns (e) and (d) by column (b). Finally, the total effect in column (i) is computed by dividing the difference between columns (e) and (b) by column (b).

The decompositions shown in tables 4.2, 4.3, and 4.4 are useful because they yield information about the relative sizes of the substitution, ordinary income, and extra income effects. For example, table 4.2's decomposition of the effect of tax reform on wage expenditures shows that all three effects are positive, as expected. Also, even without the extra income effect (2.26 percent), the 1986 tax reform could be expected to increase wage quantities substantially (that is, by 7.15 percent, the sum of the substitution and ordinary income effects).

Table 4.3 shows that the substitution effect of the 1986 tax reform on real pension expenditures is very large (−18.46 percent), and dominates the ordinary income effect (13.87 percent). Only because the extra income effect is fairly large (5.47 percent) does the computed total effect emerge as positive (0.88 percent). It follows that the effect of tax reform on real pension expenditures depends on whether corporations or households bear the burden of the corporation income tax. As discussed above, the decreased importance of the personal income tax and the increased importance of the corporate income tax under the 1986 tax reform could raise workers' money compensation if the incidence of the corporation income tax is not shifted to workers through lower wages or to consumers through higher prices. Even if we assume that corporations bear the burden of the tax, we must conclude that the 1986 tax reform has only slightly increased real pension expenditures (0.88 percent). Accordingly, it seems safest to conclude that the 1986 tax reform resulted in a small change in pension expenditures—probably a decrease if households share the burden of the increase in the corporation income tax.

Table 4.4's decomposition of the effect of tax reform on real health insurance expenditures shows that the 1986 tax reform can be expected to increase health insurance expenditures, even absent the extra income effect. The substitution effect, although negative (−6.05 percent) is dominated by the ordinary income effect (11.88 percent). It follows that

**Figure 4.1.   Effect of the 1986 tax reform on
wages and pensions decomposed.**

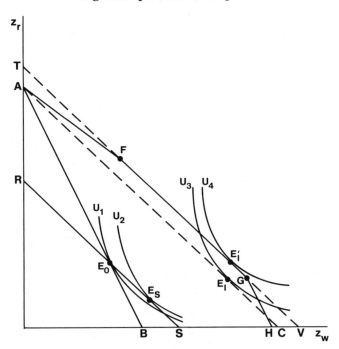

the 1986 tax reform can be expected to lead to increased pressure on the
demand for health insurance.

4. *Graphical Treatment of the Decomposition.* Figure 4.1 illustrates
the decomposition discussed above by showing graphically the effects of
the 1986 tax reform on pension quantities. The axes of figure 4.1 show
the quantities of (real expenditures on) wage compensation (z_w) and
pension compensation (z_r). The budget constraint facing the worker
before tax reform is *AB*, which is shown for simplicity as a linear
constraint. The worker maximizes well-being by choosing the mix of
compensation shown by point E_0. The 1986 tax reform results in a new
budget constraint, shown as the kinked constraint *AFGH*. This budget

constraint implies lower marginal tax rates on wages than does AB — that is, a more favorable tradeoff between pension contributions and wages, which we would expect to result in more wage compensation and less pension compensation. $AFGH$ is kinked to show the increasing marginal tax rates faced by workers as wage compensation increases.

The post-tax-reform equilibrium is shown at point E'_I. The worker has optimized by locating on segment FG of the new post-tax-reform budget constraint. The movement from the original equilibrium E_0, to E'_I, can be divided into three parts, which correspond to the three-way decomposition shown in tables 4.2, 4.3 and 4.4. First, we can show the substitution effect by pivoting the budget constraint through E_0 until it is parallel to line segment FG. This yields budget constraint RS. Given her preferences, if the worker faced RS as a constraint, she would optimize by locating at point E_S. The movement from E_0 to E_S represents the pure substitution effect of the tax reform on the worker's choice of wages and pensions.

Second, we can show the ordinary income effect by shifting RS outward in a parallel manner until the vertical intercept passes through point A. This yields budget constraint AC. Again given her preferences, if the worker faced AC as a constraint, she would optimize by locating at point E_I. The movement from E_S to E_I represents the ordinary income effect of the tax reform.

Finally, because of the nonlinearity of the new budget constraint, $AFGH$, there is an extra income effect, which is represented by the movement from E_I to E'_I. In effect, the tax reform has increased the worker's disposable money income, which results in a parallel shift outward of the budget constraint.

The quantity changes shown in figure 4.1 are as we would expect from the familiar indifference curve analysis. The substitution effect unambiguously increases wage compensation and reduces pensions. The income effects have an ambiguous effect — in this case the income effects are both positive, although the extra income effect on wages is only slightly so.

Note also that budget shares can be read from figure 4.1. For example, at the initial equilibrium E_0, the share of compensation received as pensions equals distance E_0B divided by distance AB.

5. *Revenue Effects*. Revenue effects of all tax policy changes considered in this chapter are collected in appendix table A4.1. The top panel of table A4.1 shows the aggregate revenue effect of the 1986 tax reform, and also the tax reform's effects on workers in low-wage, medium-wage, and high-wage industries. The simulation shows an effect of the tax reform that is nearly proportional across industries. The aggregate effect of the tax reform is to decrease revenues from the federal personal income tax by over 21 percent. This estimate seems in accord with the intent of the tax reform (to reduce the importance of the personal income tax and increase the importance of the corporation income tax).

Summary of the Effects of the 1986 Tax Reform

The effects of the 1986 tax reform on compensation can be summarized as follows. First, and most important, the tax reform is responsible for significant increases in real health insurance expenditures and in the share of compensation taken as health insurance. This increase in health insurance seems at first paradoxical: It occurs in spite of the reduced incentive to receive compensation as health insurance that results from lower marginal tax rates on wages. *The increase in health insurance is attributable to two factors: the large income effects of the tax reform, and the inelastic demand for health insurance.* Regarding the former, the increase in health insurance is predicted even without any of the increase in households' disposable incomes that would occur if corporations bore the burden of the increased corporation income tax under the tax reform. Regarding the latter, the inelastic demand for health insurance contributions implies that raising the tax-price of health insurance increases the share of compensation demanded as health insurance.

Second, the tax reform is responsible for significantly increasing real wage expenditures. The increase in wage compensation results because of the reduced tax-price of wages implied by lower marginal tax rates.

Nevertheless, the *share* of compensation received as wages is little affected by the tax reform due to the relatively larger increase in health insurance compensation.

Third, the 1986 tax reform is responsible for shifting the mix of compensation away from pensions and toward health insurance. (As just noted, there is only an insignificant shift of the mix of compensation between wages, on the one hand, and fringe benefits taken together, on the other.)

Fourth, the simulations suggest that tax reform is responsible for a significant drop in revenues from the federal personal income tax — a drop of over 21 percent.

Fifth, the distributional effects of the tax reform appear to be quite even. The revenue effect just mentioned appears to be, in proportional terms, similar across industries. Also, the effects of the reform on compensation appear to be similar across industries. Workers in high-wage industries experience greater increases in wages than workers in low-wage industries, but other differences between high- and low-wage industries are not great.

Of these findings, the most significant are that (a) the 1986 tax reform is responsible for increasing real health insurance expenditures and an increasing share of compensation taken as health insurance, and (b) the reform is responsible for shifting the mix of compensation away from pensions and toward health insurance. The increase in health insurance occurs (as noted above) because of the income effects of tax reform, and because the demand for health insurance contributions is very inelastic, or unresponsive to changes in tax-prices. The implication is that raising the tax-price of health insurance increases the share of compensation demanded as health insurance. The shift away from pensions and toward health insurance occurs because workers are very willing to substitute back and forth between pensions and wages. That is, the demand for pensions is highly elastic, or responsive to changes in tax-prices. It follows that raising the tax-price of pensions reduces the share of compensation demanded as pension compensation.

The results of simulating the 1986 tax reform are troubling because they suggest that it will be difficult to bring down health insurance expenditures or the health insurance share of compensation. Indeed, because the 1986 tax reform has such large income effects, it increases the demand for health insurance even though it reduces the tax-price incentives to demand health insurance. The growth of health insurance expenditures has been a major concern of economists who believe that too-generous health insurance has contributed to overexpansion of the health care sector, exploding health care costs, and inefficient resource allocation. This concern will recur in the next section, which treats schemes to tax health insurance contributions.

Tax Caps on Health Insurance Contributions

Background on Taxing Health Insurance Contributions

The taxation of employer contributions to health insurance has been much discussed and debated since the 1970s. Martin Feldstein (1973) seems to have triggered the debate with his argument that excluding health insurance contributions from taxation distorts the incentive to demand health insurance, and ultimately leads to increased use of the health care system.

The arguments of Feldstein (and of others who have followed him) have both a pragmatic and a welfare-theoretic aspect. The pragmatic aspect is that the tax-favored status of health insurance is responsible for the rising cost of medical care: "the tax laws give an incentive to purchase more health insurance, and . . . health insurance encourages consumers to purchase more medical care than they would in the absence of health insurance" (Vogel 1980, p. 220). The welfare-theoretic aspect is that a tax subsidy for health insurance is inefficient: The government could provide the same amount of health care directly, finance the health care through lump-sum taxes, and have revenue left over that could be returned to taxpayers or used to buy other public goods or services.[4]

Since Feldstein raised his concern, at least three studies have appeared that estimate how taxing health contributions would alter the provision of health insurance by employers (Taylor and Wilensky 1983; Phelps 1984–85; Adamache and Sloan 1985). Although these studies are difficult to compare with each other, their results appear to be rather divergent. Adamache and Sloan (1985, pp. 53–55) find the largest impacts of taxing health insurance contributions. They conclude that taxing contributions over $1,200 would reduce health insurance contributions by 18 percent, and that taxing all health contributions would reduce those contributions by 94 percent. Taylor and Wilensky (1983) find that a moderate tax cap ($1,800 for family policies, $720 for individual policies) would reduce health insurance contributions by about 7 percent, and that taxing all health contributions would reduce those contributions by about 17 percent. In a treatment that blends theoretical and institutional issues, Phelps (1984–85) has concluded that the tax cap proposed by the Reagan administration in 1984 ($2,100 for family policies and $840 for individual policies) would fail to stem the use of basic physician and hospital services, and would fail also to raise significant revenues. His reasoning is that a moderate or high tax cap would reduce the demand only for what he calls "fringe" medical services, such as dental care, eye care, and drugs. He reasons that only a low tax cap, or taxation of all health contributions, would significantly reduce health insurance contributions and raise revenues.

A potentially important improvement to these earlier studies of a tax cap on health insurance contributions needs to be explored: the existing studies have not taken account of the presence of pensions (or other fringe benefits) in the compensation package. Doing so could be important for at least two reasons. First, the complementarity between pensions and health insurance found in chapter 3 could imply that taxing health contributions would have a significant impact on the provision of pensions by employers. Second, if a tax cap on health insurance did affect pension provision, then it would be important to take account of that effect in determining the revenue effects of taxing health contributions. Failure to do so could lead to a biased estimate of the revenues that would be raised by taxing health insurance contributions.

Most theoretical discussions of a tax cap on health insurance have implied that a tax cap would lead to significant decreases in the share of compensation taken as health insurance. However, as discussed above, consumer theory makes no prediction about how a compensated price change affects the share of a good in the consumer's budget—that is, the sign of the substitution effect in share terms is indeterminate. Consumer theory predicts only that the substitution effect—in *quantity* (or real expenditure) terms—of taxing health insurance contributions will be negative. Estimates of the substitution effect obtained in chapter 3 accord with this prediction. In addition, we know from the chapter 3 estimates that the demand for health insurance is income elastic. Since taxing health insurance both raises the price of health insurance and lowers incomes, we can predict that taxing health insurance will depress the quantity demanded of health insurance—that both the substitution and income effects of the tax will work to reduce the *quantity* of health insurance demanded (or real expenditures on health insurance). But the same intuition does not apply to the effects of taxation on health insurance *shares*. To predict the effects on shares, we need to know the full structure of preferences for compensation.

In this section, we simulate the effects of taxing health insurance contributions by the procedure outlined earlier. We first simulate the effects of treating all employer contributions to health insurance as taxable income, and then simulate the effects of treating as taxable income employer contributions to health insurance over $1,125 per year (in 1982 dollars). This latter tax cap is similar to the most restrictive of the tax caps simulated by Taylor and Wilensky (1983), short of taxing all health insurance contributions.

For each case (taxing all contributions and taxing contributions over $1,125), we offer two sets of simulations. The first are simulations *under the tax systems existing in 1969–1982*. These simulations entail constructing an algorithm that creates the relative prices of pensions and health insurance ($\widetilde{p_r/p_w}$) and ($\widetilde{p_h/p_w}$) and real income ($\widetilde{m/P^*}$) that would have prevailed in each industry and each year from 1969 through 1982 if employer contributions for health insurance had been taxed as income. (That is, we start with the tax system in effect in each year and modify the system so that the tax treatment of health insurance contributions is altered.) The simulated relative prices and income obtained in this way are then substituted into equations (4.3) and (4.4) to obtain the simulated shares of pensions and health insurance benefits ($\tilde{s}_r$ and $\tilde{s}_h$), and subsequently real expenditures on each component of compensation. As was true in the simulation of the 1986 tax reform, the demographic and other control variables (x_1 through x_K) are assumed unaffected by the change in tax treatment of health contributions, and hence are held constant in the simulation. These simulations show how taxing health insurance contributions during the 1969–1982 period would have altered fringe benefit provision in those years.

The second set of simulations are *under the 1986 tax reform*. In these, we simulate the shares and real expenditures that would be observed if health insurance contributions were taxed under the system represented by the 1986 tax reform. These shares are compared with the shares and real expenditures that would be observed under the 1986 tax reform without taxing health insurance contributions. This second set of simulations offers a picture of what could be expected if health insurance contributions were taxed under the current tax system.

Taxing All Health Insurance Contributions

1. *Simulations Under Tax Systems Existing in 1969–1982.* Table 4.5 shows how taxing all health insurance contributions under the tax systems in effect during 1969 through 1982 would have changed real expenditures on compensation, and compensation shares, in each of those years. The effects shown are in percentage terms and averaged over the full 1969–1982 period. The first panel shows the total effects of taxing health contributions, the second isolates the substitution effects, and the third shows a disaggregation of the total effects on real expenditures by industry. (See the previous discussions of decomposing the total effect into substitution and income effects, and of disaggregating by industry.)

Table 4.5 suggests that, overall during the 1969–1982 period, taxing all health insurance contributions would have reduced employers' real health insurance expenditures by over 22 percent. About three-quarters

Table 4.5 Simulated Effects of Taxing Health Insurance Contributions: Average Percentage Changes Under Tax Systems Existing 1969–1982

	Wages	Pensions	Health Insurance
Total Effects on:			
Real Expenditures	–1.8	–5.8	–22.3
Compensation Shares	0.2	–4.7	2.2
Substitution Effects on:			
Real Expenditures	1.0	2.8	–16.9
Compensation Shares	–0.2	–0.6	4.6
Total Effects on Real Expenditures, by Industry Group:			
Aggregate	–1.8	–5.8	–22.3
Low-Wage Industries	–0.7	–1.9	–20.0
Medium-Wage Industries	–1.5	–6.0	–19.9
High-Wage Industries	–2.9	–5.6	–26.2

NOTES: The figures show how treating employer contributions to health insurance as taxable income under the tax systems in effect during 1969 through 1982 would have changed real expenditures on compensation and shares of compensation. Changes are shown in annual percentage terms, averaged over the 14 years. "Total effect" refers to the sum of the substitution, ordinary income, and extra income effects. The substitution effect isolates the impact of the changing tax-price of health insurance.

of this reduction can be attributed to substitution away from health insurance as a result of a higher tax-price of health insurance (since the substitution effect accounts for 16.9 percent out of the 22.3 percent decrease). The rest of the decrease results from the negative income effect of taxing health insurance contributions.

The substitution effects of taxing health insurance on wages and pensions are positive (1.0 percent and 2.8 percent). But because of the negative income effects of taxing health insurance, the total effects on real expenditures of both wages and pensions are negative.

The simulation suggests that taxing health insurance during the 1969-1982 period would actually have *increased* the share of health insurance in total compensation. The reason is that the demand for health insurance is inelastic. Also, the share of pensions would have been lower, and the share of wages roughly constant.

The bottom panel of table 4.5 shows how taxing health insurance would have affected different groups of workers. The simulation suggests that taxing health insurance would have decreased income inequality. Workers in low-wage industries would have experienced smaller decreases in wages, pensions, and health insurance than workers in high-wage industries. But these distributional effects are not dramatic: The decrease in health insurance for workers in high-wage industries would have been 26.2 percent, compared with 20 percent for workers in low-wage industries.

Table A4.1 displays estimates of how federal personal income tax revenues would have increased if health insurance had been taxed during the 1969–1982 period (see the second panel, left column). The overall increase in revenues would have been nearly 9 percent per year. The distribution of this revenue increase would have decreased income inequality: workers in low-wage industries would have experienced a 6.9-percent increase in income taxes, whereas workers in high-wage industries would have experienced nearly a 13-percent increase.

2. *Simulations Under the 1986 Tax Reform.* Table 4.6 displays estimates of how taxing all health insurance contributions under the 1986 tax reform could be expected to alter real expenditures on compensation and compensation shares. The effects are in percentage terms, with total effects displayed in the first panel, substitution effects in the second panel, and the disaggregation of total effects by industry in the third panel.

Table 4.6 suggests that taxing all health insurance contributions would reduce employers' real health insurance expenditures by nearly 15 percent. Substitution away from health insurance as a result of a higher tax-price of health insurance accounts for most of this effect (−11.9 percent out of −14.7 percent). The negative income effect of taxing health insurance is responsible for the remainder.

The substitution effects on wages and pensions of taxing health insurance are slightly positive (0.7 percent and 0.1 percent). But the total effects on both wage and pension expendutures are negative (be-

**Table 4.6   Simulated Effects of Taxing Health Insurance Contributions:
Average Percentage Changes Under 1986 Tax Reform**

	Wages	Pensions	Health Insurance
Total Effects on:			
Real Expenditures	−0.7	−4.3	−14.7
Compensation Shares	0.1	−3.7	1.8
Substitution Effects on:			
Real Expenditures	0.7	0.1	−11.9
Compensation Shares	−0.1	−1.5	3.1
Total Effects on Real Expenditures, by Industry Group:			
Aggregate	−0.7	−4.3	−14.7
Low-Wage Industries	−0.4	−5.9	−12.8
Medium-Wage Industries	−0.5	−4.7	−13.8
High-Wage Industries	−1.1	−3.7	−15.9

NOTES: The figures show how treating employer contributions to health insurance as taxable under the 1986 tax reform would have changed real expenditures on compensation and shares of compensation. "Total effect" refers to the sum of the substitution, ordinary income, and extra income effects. The substitution effect isolates the impact of the changing tax-price of health insurance.

cause the negative income effects of taxing health insurance dominate the small positive substitution effects).

We found above that if health insurance had been taxed during the 1969–1982 period, the health insurance share of total compensation would have increased. Taxing health insurance under the 1986 tax reform also increases the health insurance share (by 1.8 percent), again because of the inelastic demand for health insurance. Pensions would fall as a share of compensation if health insurance were taxed (the substitution effect is − 1.5 percent, and the total effect is − 3.7 percent), but the share of wages would be virtually unchanged.

The distributional effects shown in the bottom panel of table 4.6 suggest that taxing health insurance under the 1986 tax reform would have similar effects on different groups of workers. Workers in low-wage industries would experience somewhat smaller decreases in wages and health insurance than workers in high-wage industries, but somewhat larger decreases in pensions. Note that the 13 percent reduction in health insurance predicted for workers in low-wage industries could turn a marginally adequate health insurance plan into an inadequate plan. Such an impact would need to be considered in appraising the desirability of taxing health insurance contributions, and could offset what may be viewed as a desirable (although small) increase in overall distributional equality.

The revenue estimates shown in table A4.1 (second panel, right column) suggest that taxing all health insurance contributions would increase personal income tax revenues by over 8 percent per year. The distribution of this revenue increase would tend to increase equality: Workers in low- and medium-wage industries would experience an increase of 7 to 8 percent in income taxes, whereas workers in high-wage industries would experience an increase of nearly 11 percent.

Tables 4.7, 4.8, and 4.9 decompose the effects of taxing health insurance into substitution, ordinary income, and extra income effects.[5] Table 4.7 shows the results of decomposing the effect of taxing health insurance on real wage expenditures, and tables 4.8 and 4.9 show the decompositions for real expenditures on pensions and health insurance. (See above for a detailed treatment of the decomposition.)

Table 4.7 shows that taxing health insurance would have virtually no impact on real wage expenditures absent the extra income effect – that is, if taxing health insurance had no effect on money disposable incomes. Even with the extra income effect, the impact of taxing health insurance on wages is small.

Table 4.8 shows that taxing health insurance has an ambiguous substitution effect on real pension expenditures. Because pensions and health insurance are weak complements in our simulation model, a compensated increase in the price of health insurance can either increase or decrease real pension expenditures. Both the ordinary and extra income effects are consistently negative, and either by itself would dominate the substitution effect. We conclude that taxing health insurance would lead to a moderate decrease in real pension expenditures.

Table 4.9 shows that taxing fringe benefits has a large substitution

Table 4.7 Simulated Effects of Taxing Health Insurance on Real Wage Expenditures

(a)	(b)	(c)	(d)	(e)	(f)	(g)	(h)	(i)
Year	Predicted	Simulated: Only Relative Prices Changed	Simulated: Relative Prices and P^* Changed	Simulated: Relative Prices, P^*, and m Changed	Substitution Effect (Percent)	Ordinary Income Effect (Percent)	Extra Income Effect (Percent)	Total Effect (Percent)
1969	13438	13503	13436	13379	0.48	-0.50	-0.42	-0.44
1970	13283	13353	13281	13216	0.53	-0.54	-0.49	-0.50
1971	13861	13937	13837	13766	0.55	-0.72	-0.51	-0.69
1972	14134	14227	14135	14057	0.66	-0.65	-0.55	-0.54
1973	14030	14118	14012	13936	0.63	-0.76	-0.54	-0.67
1974	13818	13907	13819	13744	0.64	-0.64	-0.54	-0.54
1975	13991	14080	13992	13909	0.64	-0.63	-0.59	-0.59
1976	14264	14351	14265	14177	0.61	-0.60	-0.62	-0.61
1977	14381	14488	14384	14289	0.74	-0.72	-0.66	-0.64
1978	14402	14496	14389	14274	0.65	-0.74	-0.80	-0.89
1979	14311	14413	14314	14220	0.71	-0.69	-0.66	-0.64
1980	14271	14366	14252	14156	0.67	-0.80	-0.67	-0.81
1981	14241	14333	14221	14123	0.65	-0.79	-0.69	-0.83
1982	14374	14493	14360	14253	0.83	-0.93	-0.74	-0.84
Mean	14154	14248	14144	14054	0.66	-0.73	-0.64	-0.71

NOTES: Columns (b) through (e) show real wage expenditures by year (these may also be thought of as quantities or constant dollar expenditures). The predicted figures (column (b)) provide the base for our comparisons, showing wage expenditures predicted by our model in each year if the 1986 tax reform (with health insurance untaxed) had been in effect. Columns (c), (d), and (e) show the simulated effects of taxing health insurance under the 1986 tax reform. Column (c) shows wage expenditures if only the substitution effect occurred, column (d) shows wage expenditures if both substitution and ordinary income effects occurred, and column (e) shows wage expenditures if substitution, ordinary income, and extra income effects occurred.

Columns (f) through (i) show substitution, ordinary income, extra income, and total effects in percentage terms, and are computed from the figures in columns (b) through (e).

Table 4.8 Simulated Effects of Taxing Health Insurance on Real Pension Expenditures

(a)	(b)	(c)	(d)	(e)	(f)	(g)	(h)	(i)
Year	Predicted	Simulated: Only Relative Prices Changed	Simulated: Relative Prices and $P*$ Changed	Simulated: Relative Prices, $P*$, and m Changed	Substitution Effect (Percent)	Ordinary Income Effect (Percent)	Extra Income Effect (Percent)	Total Effect (Percent)
1969	623	614	603	592	-1.44	-1.77	-1.77	-4.98
1970	633	625	613	601	-1.26	-1.90	-1.90	-5.06
1971	770	767	749	736	-0.39	-2.34	-1.69	-4.42
1972	840	833	816	801	-0.83	-2.02	-1.79	-4.64
1973	846	843	823	808	-0.35	-2.36	-1.77	-4.49
1974	849	843	826	811	-0.71	-2.00	-1.77	-4.48
1975	952	947	929	911	-0.53	-1.89	-1.89	-4.31
1976	1053	1048	1029	1010	-0.47	-1.80	-1.80	-4.08
1977	1083	1080	1057	1037	-0.28	-2.12	-1.85	-4.25
1978	1120	1128	1096	1075	0.71	-2.86	-1.88	-4.02
1979	1124	1120	1098	1076	-0.36	-1.96	-1.96	-4.27
1980	1138	1149	1114	1091	0.97	-3.08	-2.02	-4.13
1981	1170	1181	1146	1122	0.94	-2.99	-2.05	-4.10
1982	1262	1267	1234	1207	0.40	-2.61	-2.14	-4.36
Mean	1033	1034	1009	989	0.10	-2.42	-1.94	-4.26

NOTES: Columns (b) through (e) show real pension expenditures by year (these may also be thought of as quantities or constant dollar expenditures). The predicted figures (column (b)) provide the base for our comparisons, showing pension expenditures predicted by our model in each year if the 1986 tax reform (with health insurance untaxed) had been in effect. Columns (c), (d), and (e) show the simulated effects of taxing health insurance under the 1986 tax reform. Column (c) shows pension expenditures if only the substitution effect occurred, column (d) shows pension expenditures if both substitution and ordinary income effects occurred, and column (e) shows pension expenditures if substitution, ordinary income, and extra income effects occurred.

Columns (f) through (i) show substitution, ordinary income, extra income, and total effects in percentage terms, and are computed from the figures in columns (b) through (e).

Table 4.9 Simulated Effects of Taxing Health Insurance on Real Health Insurance Expenditures

(a) Year	(b) Predicted	(c) Simulated: Only Relative Prices Changed	(d) Simulated: Relative Prices and P^* Changed	(e) Simulated: Relative Prices, P^*, and m Changed	(f) Substitution Effect (Percent)	(g) Ordinary Income Effect (Percent)	(h) Extra Income Effect (Percent)	(i) Total Effect (Percent)
1969	557	496	490	484	-10.95	-1.08	-1.08	-13.11
1970	609	542	534	527	-11.00	-1.31	-1.15	-13.46
1971	656	582	572	565	-11.28	-1.52	-1.07	-13.87
1972	627	556	547	540	-11.32	-1.44	-1.12	-13.88
1973	665	589	579	571	-11.43	-1.50	-1.20	-14.14
1974	808	715	705	695	-11.51	-1.24	-1.24	-13.99
1975	985	870	857	845	-11.68	-1.32	-1.22	-14.21
1976	1055	932	918	904	-11.66	-1.33	-1.33	-14.31
1977	933	824	810	798	-11.68	-1.50	-1.29	-14.47
1978	1028	906	888	875	-11.87	-1.75	-1.26	-14.88
1979	1153	1016	1000	985	-11.88	-1.39	-1.30	-14.57
1980	1199	1055	1035	1019	-12.01	-1.67	-1.33	-15.01
1981	1185	1042	1023	1006	-12.07	-1.60	-1.43	-15.11
1982	1162	1019	998	982	-12.31	-1.81	-1.38	-15.49
Mean	985	868	853	840	-11.88	-1.52	-1.32	-14.72

NOTES: Columns (b) through (e) show real health insurance expenditures by year (these may also be thought of as quantities or constant dollar expenditures). The predicted figures (column (b)) provide the base for our comparisons, showing health insurance expenditures predicted by our model in each year if the 1986 tax reform (with health insurance untaxed) had been in effect. Columns (c), (d), and (e) show the simulated effects of taxing health insurance under the 1986 tax reform. Column (c) shows health insurance expenditures if only the substitution effect occurred, column (d) shows health insurance expenditures if both substitution and ordinary income effects occurred, and column (e) shows health insurance expenditures if substitution, ordinary income, and extra income effects occurred.

Columns (f) through (i) show substitution, ordinary income, extra income, and total effects in percentage terms, and are computed from the figures in columns (b) through (e).

effect on health insurance (−11.9 percent). Income effects, although also negative, are relatively minor. It follows that taxing health insurance would reduce the demand for health insurance by nearly 15 percent. This is remarkably close to Taylor and Wilensky's (1983) estimate of the effect of taxing health insurance−a reduction of 17 percent.[6]

A Low Tax Cap on Health Insurance Contributions

1. *Simulations Under Tax Systems Existing in 1969–1982.* Table 4.10 summarizes how taxing health insurance contributions over $1,125 per year (in 1982 dollars) would have affected compensation during the 1969–1982 period. (Such a policy is often referred to as a low tax cap on health insurance contributions.) A comparison of table 4.10 with table 4.5 shows that the differences between taxing all health insurance and taxing only contributions over $1,125 are strictly a matter of magnitude−all effects have the same direction. The effects of the low tax cap tend to be about one-half the size of the effects of taxing all benefits. (This is simply a matter of the level of the tax cap we have simulated.)

Aside from the smaller magnitude of effects under the low tax cap, one further difference between a low tax cap and taxing all health insurance contributions is worth noting: The distributional impacts of the low tax cap are more equalizing than are those of taxing all benefits. This can be seen in the third panel of table 4.10, where the reduction in health insurance experienced by workers in high-wage industries is well above the average for all workers. Also, the revenue increases resulting from a low tax cap are concentrated on workers in high-wage industries, as can be seen from table A4.1 (third panel, left column). Whereas workers in low- and medium-wage industries experience very small income tax increases, workers in high-wage industries experience increases over 5 percent.

2. *Simulations Under the 1986 Tax Reform.* Effects of a low tax cap on health insurance under the 1986 tax reform are shown in table 4.11.

Table 4.10 Simulated Effects of a Low Tax Cap on Health Insurance Contributions: Average Percentage Changes Under Tax Systems Existing 1969–1982

	Wages	Pensions	Health Insurance
Total Effects on:			
Real Expenditures	–0.4	–2.6	–13.9
Compensation Shares	0.1	–1.8	0.7
Substitution Effects on:			
Real Expenditures	0.7	1.6	–11.3
Compensation Shares	–0.1	–0.4	1.8
Total Effects on Real Expenditures, by Industry Group:			
Aggregate	–0.4	–2.6	–13.9
Low-Wage Industries	–0.0	–0.6	–2.5
Medium-Wage Industries	–0.0	–1.5	–7.4
High-Wage Industries	–1.1	–3.7	–22.3

NOTES: The figures show how taxing annual employer contributions to health insurance over $1,125 (in 1982 dollars) under the tax systems in effect during 1969 through 1982 would have changed real expenditures on compensation and shares of compensation. Changes are shown in annual percentage terms averaged over the 14 years. "Total effect" refers to the sum of the substitution, ordinary income, and extra income effects. The substitution effect isolates the impact of the changing tax-price of health insurance.

Comparing table 4.11 with table 4.6 shows again that the effects of taxing health insurance contributions over $1,125 are in the same direction as the effects of taxing all health contributions. The effects of the low tax cap are simply smaller.

A more significant difference between the low tax cap and taxing all benefits under the 1986 tax reform is that (as under the 1969–1982 tax systems) the distributional impacts of the low tax cap are more equalizing. The reduction in health insurance experienced by workers in high-wage industries is far greater than the reduction experienced by other workers (table 4.11, third panel). Also, workers in high-wage industries experience a far greater increase in federal personal income taxes than do workers in low- and medium-wage industries (table A4.1, third panel, right column).

**Table 4.11 Simulated Effects of a Low Tax Cap on
Health Insurance Contributions: Average Percentage
Changes Under 1986 Tax Reform**

	Wages	Pensions	Health Insurance
Total Effects on:			
Real Expenditures	-0.1	-1.7	-8.7
Compensation Shares	0.0	-1.5	0.4
Substitution Effects on:			
Real Expenditures	0.4	0.2	-7.4
Compensation Shares	-0.0	-0.6	1.0
Total Effects on Real Expenditures, by Industry Group:			
Aggregate	-0.1	-1.7	-8.7
Low-Wage Industries	-0.0	-0.5	-1.7
Medium-Wage Industries	-0.0	-0.9	-5.1
High-Wage Industries	-0.3	-2.5	-13.5

NOTES: The figures show how taxing annual employer contributions to health insurance over $1,125 (in 1982 dollars) under the 1986 tax reform would change real expenditures on compensation and shares of compensation. "Total effect" refers to the sum of the substitution, ordinary income, and extra income effects. The substitution effect isolates the impact of the changing tax-price of health insurance.

Summary of the Effects of Taxing Health Insurance

The effects of treating employer contributions to health insurance as taxable income can be summarized as follows. First, taxing health insurance under the current tax system can be expected to substantially reduce employers' real expenditures on health insurance. Our simulations suggest that taxing all health insurance contributions would reduce real health insurance expenditures by nearly 15 percent (table 4.6), whereas taxing all contributions in excess of $1,125 per year (in 1982 dollars) would reduce real health insurance expenditures by nearly 9 percent (table 4.11).

Second, real expenditures on wages and pensions would also fall if health insurance contributions were taxed. These decreases result because taxing health insurance would reduce real incomes, which would lead in turn to reductions in both wages and pensions.

Third, the simulations suggest that taxing all health insurance contributions would increase revenues from the federal personal income tax by over 8 percent annually, and that taxing health contributions over $1,125 would increase income tax revenues by 1.5 percent (table A4.1).

Fourth, the distributional effects of taxing *all* health insurance contributions are not dramatic. Workers in low-wage industries would experience somewhat smaller decreases in wages and health insurance than workers in high-wage industries. Also, workers in high-wage industries would experience somewhat larger increases in their income tax bills. But the differences among different groups of workers are not great.

In contrast, the distributional effects of taxing health insurance contributions over $1,125 are significant. Under the low tax cap, workers in high-wage industries would experience a 13.5 percent decrease in health insurance, whereas workers in low- and medium-wage industries would experience a decrease of only 2 to 5 percent. Also, the income taxes of workers in high-wage industries would rise by over 4 percent, whereas the income taxes of other workers would rise by under 1 percent.

The picture that emerges from our simulations is that a tax cap on health insurance would both reduce employers' real health insurance expenditures and have distributional effects that appear to increase income equality. The low tax cap on health insurance that we have examined would raise far less revenue than would taxing all health insurance — it would raise income tax revenues by only 1.5 percent. But it would nevertheless limit the extent to which health insurance contributions escape taxation and would likewise limit further erosion of the tax base as health insurance costs and contributions increase.

Taxing All Fringe Benefit Contributions

Why Tax All Benefits?

Students and critics of the U.S. retirement income system have followed the lead of the health economists and advocated taxing employer contributions to private pensions as well as to health insurance.

Alicia Munnell has been perhaps the leading proponent of taxing pension contributions, arguing that the tax-favored treatment of pensions (as well as health insurance) has led to both erosion of the income and payroll tax bases and a more regressive tax system (Munnell 1984, 1985). As the growth of voluntary fringe benefits has slowed (Woodbury and Huang 1988), these arguments have lost some of their force. But more recently, Munnell (1988a, 1988b) has generally criticized the private pension system in the U.S. on the grounds that it covers too small a proportion of households, reduces mobility of the workforce, and provides benefits whose real purchasing power is vulnerable to inflation. She advocates expansion of the public pension system – OASI – and contraction of the private pension system. Taxing employer contributions to private pensions is clearly one possible way of reducing the importance of private pensions in the U.S.

It is also possible to make the same type of welfare-theoretic case for taxing pension contributions that health economists have made regarding health insurance: A tax subsidy for pension contributions can be seen as inefficient in that the government could provide a retirement income of equal value that would be financed out of lump-sum taxes, and still have revenue left over. But the pragmatic case for taxing health insurance – that the tax-favored status of health insurance distorts incentives to use health care and leads ultimately to an inefficiently large health care sector – cannot be applied to pensions. To our knowledge, no one has argued that saving in general or saving for retirement is excessive. On the contrary, there is much concern about the relatively low rate of saving in the United States, and about the slow growth of that capital stock and aggregate output that has resulted (Seidman 1990). Nor has anyone argued that incomes of retirees are excessive.

The case for taxing pension contributions seems weaker *a priori* than the case for taxing health insurance. Nevertheless, enough serious consideration has been given to the policy option of taxing all fringe benefits to make taxation of pension contributions a serious issue. Indeed, even with the current administration's aversion to tax increases, the issue of taxing pension contributions continues to be discussed (Birnbaum 1989).

Accordingly, in this section we discuss simulations of the impacts of treating employer contributions to both pensions and health insurance as taxable income. To our knowledge, these are the first such simulations, so there are no previous estimates with which to compare them. We use the same procedure as with our simulations of taxing health insurance. Also as with taxing health insurance, we offer two sets of simulations. The first, simulations *under the tax systems existing in 1969–1982*, show how taxing pensions and health insurance during the 1969–1982 period would have altered fringe benefit provision in those years. The second, simulations *under the 1986 tax reform*, show what could be expected if pensions and health insurance were taxed under the current tax system.

Results of Simulating a Tax on All Fringe Benefits

1. *Simulations Under Tax Systems Existing in 1969–1982.* How would compensation have changed if all fringe benefits had been taxed during 1969 through 1982? Table 4.12 displays results of our simulation and offers some answers. The effects on real expenditures on compensation and on compensation shares are all shown in percentage terms and averaged over the 1969–1982 period. As in previous summary tables, the first panel shows total effects, the second isolates the substitution effects, and the third shows a disaggregation of the total effects by industry. (See our earlier discussions of decomposing the total effect into substitution and income effects and of disaggregating by industry.)

The simulation in table 4.12 suggests that treating all employer contributions to pensions and health insurance as taxable income would have dramatically changed the pattern of compensation during the 1969–1982 period. Pension benefits would have been lower by 64 percent, and health insurance benefits lower by nearly 28 percent. Most of these cuts can be attributed to substitution away from fringe benefits as a result of a higher tax-price of fringes: the substitution effect accounts for 84 percent ($-53.9/-64.1$) of the pension decrease and for 65 percent ($-18.2/-27.9$) of the health insurance decrease. The re-

**Table 4.12 Simulated Effects of Taxing All Fringe Benefit
Contributions: Average Percentage Changes
Under Tax Systems Existing 1969–1982**

	Wages	Pensions	Health Insurance
Total Effects on:			
Real Expenditures	–0.8	–64.1	–27.9
Compensation Shares	3.0	–53.9	–2.4
Substitution Effects on:			
Real Expenditures	4.3	–53.9	–18.2
Compensation Shares	2.4	–46.1	2.4
Total Effects on Real Expenditures, by Industry Group:			
Aggregate	–0.8	–64.1	–27.9
Low-Wage Industries	0.8	–81.1	–19.8
Medium-Wage Industries	–0.2	–70.2	–24.9
High-Wage Industries	–3.0	–57.2	–32.7

NOTES: The figures show how treating employer contributions to both pensions and health insurance as taxable income under the tax systems in effect during 1969 through 1982 would have changed real expenditures on compensation and shares of compensation. Changes are shown in annual percentage terms, averaged over the 14 years. "Total effect" refers to the sum of the substitution, ordinary income, and extra income effects. The substitution effect isolates the impact of the changing tax-price of pensions and health insurance relative to wages.

mainder of the decreases result from the negative income effect of taxing fringe benefits.

The substitution effect on wages is positive (4.3 percent), but is dominated by the negative income effect of taxing fringe benefits. Hence, the total effect of taxing fringe benefits on wage compensation is negative.

Taxing pensions and health insurance during the 1969–1982 period would also have dramatically decreased the *share* of pensions in total compensation. But the substitution effect on the health insurance *share* is actually positive (2.4 percent). The reason is that the demand for health insurance is highly inelastic. The total effect on the health insurance share is negative (−2.4 percent) only because of the negative income effects of taxing all fringe benefits.

The distributional effects of taxing all fringe benefits can be seen in the bottom panel of table 4.12. Although workers in low-wage industries would have experienced smaller (or no) reductions in wages and health insurance than workers in high-wage industries, workers in low-wage industries would have experienced *larger* cuts in pensions than workers in higher wage industries. This is a potentially troubling distributional effect of taxing all fringe benefits.

Table A4.1 shows that, if all fringe benefits had been taxed during the 1969–1982 period, federal personal income tax revenues would have been greater by 19 percent annually (bottom panel, left column). The burden of this revenue increase would have fallen more heavily on workers in high-wage industries (who would have paid nearly 30 percent more in income taxes) than on other workers (who would have paid only 13 to 15 percent more).

2. *Simulations Under the 1986 Tax Reform.* How would the pattern of compensation change if all fringe benefit contributions were taxed under the current tax system? The results of our simulation, displayed in table 4.13, suggest that taxing all fringe benefit contributions would reduce employers' real pension expenditures by nearly one-half, and would reduce real health insurance expenditures by over 20 percent. Substitution away from pensions and health insurance as a result of the higher tax-price of fringe benefits accounts for most of these effects (−38.7 percent out of −48.8 percent in the case of pensions, −12.1 percent out of −20.1 percent in the case of health insurance). The negative income effect of taxing all fringe benefits is responsible for the remainder of the decreases.

The distributional effects shown in the bottom panel of table 4.13 suggest that taxing all fringe benefits under the current system would have different effects on different groups of workers. Workers in all industries would make dramatic substitutions away from both pensions and health insurance. Workers in low-wage industries would experience larger declines in pensions than would workers in other industries, but smaller declines in health insurance and wages.

The revenue estimates shown in table A4.1 (bottom panel, right

Table 4.13   Simulated Effects of Taxing All Fringe Benefit
Contributions: Average Percentage Changes
Under 1986 Tax Reform

	Wages	Pensions	Health Insurance
Total Effects on:			
Real Expenditures	-0.4	-48.8	-20.1
Compensation Shares	2.2	-39.3	-1.6
Substitution Effects on:			
Real Expenditures	3.4	-38.7	-12.1
Compensation Shares	1.7	-33.8	1.4
Total Effects on Real Expenditures, by Industry Group:			
Aggregate	-0.4	-48.8	-20.1
Low-Wage Industries	-0.9	-68.4	-15.9
Medium-Wage Industries	-0.7	-52.3	-16.7
High-Wage Industries	-2.8	-42.9	-23.9

NOTES: The figures show how treating employer contributions to both pensions and health insurance as taxable income under the 1986 tax reform would change real expenditures on compensation and shares of compensation. "Total effect" refers to the sum of the substitution, ordinary income, and extra income effects. The substitution effect isolates the impact of the changing tax-price of pensions and health insurance relative to wages.

column) suggest that taxing all fringe benefit contributions under the current system would increase personal income tax revenues by over 17 percent annually. The distribution of this revenue increase would tend to decrease income inequality: workers in low- and medium-wage industries would experience an increase of 14 to 15 percent in income taxes, whereas workers in high-wage industries would experience an increase of nearly 26 percent.

Tables 4.14, 4.15, and 4.16 decompose the effects of taxing all fringe benefits into substitution, ordinary income, and extra income effects.[7] Table 4.14 shows the decomposition of the total effect on wages, table 4.15 shows the pension decomposition, and table 4.16 shows the health insurance decomposition.

Table 4.14 shows why taxing all fringe benefits would have almost no net impact on wage quantities: the positive substitution effect is approximately offset by negative ordinary and extra income effects.

Table 4.14 Simulated Effects of Taxing All Fringe Benefits on Real Wage Expenditures

(a)	(b)	(c)	(d)	(e)	(f)	(g)	(h)	(i)
Year	Predicted	Simulated: Only Relative Prices Changed	Simulated: Relative Prices and $P*$ Changed	Simulated: Relative Prices, $P*$, and m Changed	Substitution Effect (Percent)	Ordinary Income Effect (Percent)	Extra Income Effect (Percent)	Total Effect (Percent)
1969	13438	13813	13679	13559	2.79	-1.00	-0.89	0.90
1970	13283	13662	13523	13391	2.85	-1.05	-0.99	0.81
1971	13861	14277	14095	13949	3.00	-1.31	-1.05	0.63
1972	14134	14578	14358	14198	3.14	-1.56	-1.13	0.45
1973	14030	14470	14262	14100	3.14	-1.48	-1.15	0.50
1974	13818	14256	14063	13898	3.17	-1.40	-1.19	0.58
1975	13991	14451	14213	14026	3.29	-1.70	-1.34	0.25
1976	14264	14741	14425	14224	3.34	-2.22	-1.41	-0.28
1977	14381	14878	14473	14259	3.46	-2.82	-1.49	-0.85
1978	14402	14902	14481	14264	3.47	-2.92	-1.51	-0.96
1979	14311	14812	14395	14184	3.50	-2.91	-1.47	-0.89
1980	14271	14778	14369	14154	3.55	-2.87	-1.51	-0.82
1981	14241	14747	14335	14114	3.55	-2.89	-1.55	-0.89
1982	14374	14923	14497	14258	3.82	-2.96	-1.66	-0.81
Mean	14154	14635	14300	14103	3.40	-2.37	-1.39	-0.36

NOTES: Columns (b) through (e) show real wage expenditures by year (these may also be thought of as quantities or constant dollar expenditures). The predicted figures (column (b)) provide the base for our comparisons, showing wage expenditures predicted by our model in each year if the 1986 tax reform (with fringe benefits untaxed) had been in effect. Columns (c), (d), and (e) show the simulated effects of taxing pensions and health insurance under the 1986 tax reform. Column (c) shows wage expenditures if only the substitution effect occurred, column (d) shows wage expenditures if both substitution and ordinary income effects occurred, and column (e) shows wage expenditures if substitution, ordinary income, and extra income effects occurred.

Columns (f) through (i) show substitution, ordinary income, extra income, and total effects in percentage terms, and are computed from the figures in columns (b) through (e).

Table 4.15   Simulated Effects of Taxing All Fringe Benefits on Real Pension Expenditures

(a)	(b)	(c)	(d)	(e)	(f)	(g)	(h)	(i)
Year	Predicted	Simulated: Only Relative Prices Changed	Simulated: Relative Prices and P^* Changed	Simulated: Relative Prices, P^*, and m Changed	Substitution Effect (Percent)	Ordinary Income Effect (Percent)	Extra Income Effect (Percent)	Total Effect (Percent)
1969	623	300	283	268	-51.85	-2.73	-2.41	-56.98
1970	633	312	293	276	-50.71	-3.00	-2.69	-56.40
1971	770	419	393	373	-45.58	-3.38	-2.60	-51.56
1972	840	470	433	410	-44.05	-4.40	-2.74	-51.19
1973	846	480	447	423	-43.26	-3.90	-2.84	-50.00
1974	849	487	452	427	-42.64	-4.12	-2.94	-49.71
1975	952	569	525	495	-40.23	-4.62	-3.15	-48.00
1976	1053	650	585	551	-38.27	-6.17	-3.23	-47.67
1977	1083	674	584	549	-37.77	-8.31	-3.23	-49.31
1978	1120	705	611	574	-37.05	-8.39	-3.30	-48.75
1979	1124	709	616	579	-36.92	-8.27	-3.29	-48.49
1980	1138	721	628	589	-36.64	-8.17	-3.43	-48.24
1981	1170	748	652	612	-36.07	-8.21	-3.42	-47.69
1982	1262	812	716	670	-35.66	-7.61	-3.65	-46.91
Mean	1033	633	562	529	-38.72	-6.87	-3.19	-48.79

NOTES: Columns (b) through (e) show real pension expenditures by year (these may also be thought of as quantities or constant dollar expenditures). The predicted figures (column (b)) provide the base for our comparisons, showing pension expenditures predicted by our model in each year if the 1986 tax reform (with fringe benefits untaxed) had been in effect. Columns (c), (d), and (e) show the simulated effects of taxing pensions and health insurance under the 1986 tax reform. Column (c) shows pension expenditures if only the substitution effect occurred, column (d) shows pension expenditures if both substitution and ordinary income effects occurred, and column (e) shows pension expenditures if substitution, ordinary income, and extra income effects occurred.
   Columns (f) through (i) show substitution, ordinary income, extra income, and total effects in percentage terms, and are computed from the figures in columns (b) through (e).

Table 4.16 Simulated Effects of Taxing All Fringe Benefits on Real Health Insurance Expenditures

(a) Year	(b) Predicted	(c) Simulated: Only Relative Prices Changed	(d) Simulated: Relative Prices and P* Changed	(e) Simulated: Relative Prices, P*, and m Changed	(f) Substitution Effect (Percent)	(g) Ordinary Income Effect (Percent)	(h) Extra Income Effect (Percent)	(i) Total Effect (Percent)
1969	557	490	477	466	-12.03	-2.33	-1.97	-16.34
1970	609	536	522	509	-11.99	-2.30	-2.13	-16.42
1971	656	577	559	544	-12.04	-2.74	-2.29	-17.07
1972	627	551	531	516	-12.12	-3.19	-2.39	-17.70
1973	665	585	564	549	-12.03	-3.16	-2.26	-17.44
1974	808	711	687	668	-12.00	-2.97	-2.35	-17.33
1975	985	866	832	806	-12.08	-3.45	-2.64	-18.17
1976	1055	928	879	850	-12.04	-4.64	-2.75	-19.43
1977	933	821	764	738	-12.00	-6.11	-2.79	-20.90
1978	1028	904	838	809	-12.06	-6.42	-2.82	-21.30
1979	1153	1014	941	909	-12.06	-6.33	-2.78	-21.16
1980	1199	1054	980	947	-12.09	-6.17	-2.75	-21.02
1981	1185	1041	968	935	-12.15	-6.16	-2.78	-21.10
1982	1162	1020	949	915	-12.22	-6.11	-2.93	-21.26
Mean	985	866	813	787	-12.08	-5.38	-2.64	-20.10

NOTES: Columns (b) through (e) show real health insurance expenditures by year (these may also be thought of as quantities or constant dollar expenditures). The predicted figures (column (b)) provide the base for our comparisons, showing health insurance expenditures predicted by our model in each year if the 1986 tax reform (with fringe benefits untaxed) had been in effect. Columns (c), (d), and (e) show the simulated effects of taxing pensions and health insurance under the 1986 tax reform. Column (c) shows health insurance expenditures if only the substitution effect occurred, column (d) shows health insurance expenditures if both substitution and ordinary income effects occurred, and column (e) shows health insurance expenditures if substitution, ordinary income, and extra income effects occurred.

Columns (f) through (i) show substitution, ordinary income, extra income, and total effects in percentage terms, and are computed from the figures in columns (b) through (e).

Table 4.15 shows that, even in the absence of negative income effects, taxing all fringe benefits would lead to a large decline in employer provision of pensions: the substitution effect alone implies a decrease of nearly 39 percent in pension provision by employers.

Table 4.16 shows that the substitution effect on health insurance is weaker than on pensions: absent the negative income effects of taxing all fringe benefits, health insurance provision would fall by only 12 percent. The reason for this smaller substitution effect in the case of health insurance is that the elasticity of substitution between wages and health insurance is lower than between wages and pensions—health insurance is not as good a substitute for wages as are pensions.

Summary of the Effects of Taxing All Fringe Benefits

The effects of treating all employer contributions to pensions and health insurance as taxable income are quite dramatic. First, our simulations indicate that taxing all fringe benefits under the current system would lead to enormous reductions in employers' real expenditures on both pensions and health insurance: Pension provision would be cut by nearly 50 percent, and health insurance provision by over 20 percent (table 4.13).

Second, real wage expenditures would also fall (but far less than pensions or health insurance) if all fringe benefits were taxed. This small decrease results because taxing all fringe benefits would reduce real incomes, which would lead in turn to reduced real wage expenditures.

Third, taxing all fringe benefits would lead to a major shift in the mix of compensation away from pensions and health insurance and toward wages. The share of compensation received as pensions would be most affected—our simulations suggest a decrease in the pension share of nearly 40 percent.

Fourth, the simulations suggest that taxing all health insurance contributions would increase revenues from the federal personal income tax by over 17 percent annually (table A4.1). Also, the distribution of this tax increase would tend to increase income equality. Workers in low--

wage industries would experience income tax increases of 14 to 15 percent, whereas workers in high-wage industries would experience tax increases of nearly 26 percent.

The interesting question is: why are pensions devastated by taxing all fringe benefits, whereas health insurance is cut by only 20 percent? The answer is that pensions and wages are far better substitutes than are health insurance and wages. It follows that when pensions are taxed, workers are readily willing to substitute wages for pensions. Although they are also willing to substitute wages for health insurance, the drive to do so is not nearly as strong.

If our simulations of the effects of taxing all fringe benefits are accurate, then reforming the tax system so that all fringe benefits are taxed would very likely be politically infeasible. If employers and workers are aware of the incentives they face — and comfortable with the status quo — then major change is unlikely.

146

Table A4.1 Simulated Effects of Policy Changes
on Federal Personal Income Tax Revenues

Policy	Percentage Change in Revenue	
	Under Tax Systems 1969–1982	Under 1986 Tax Reform
1986 Tax Reform:		
Aggregate	−21.2	−
Low-Wage Industry	−21.9	−
Medium-Wage Industry	−19.8	−
High-Wage Industry	−22.8	−
Taxing Health Insurance Contributions:		
Aggregate	8.9	8.3
Low-Wage Industry	6.9	7.7
Medium-Wage Industry	7.2	6.8
High-Wage Industry	12.8	10.8
Low Tax Cap on Health Insurance:		
Aggregate	2.0	1.5
Low-Wage Industry	0.0	0.2
Medium-Wage Industry	0.6	0.6
High-Wage Industry	5.3	4.3
Taxing All Benefits:		
Aggregate	19.0	17.6
Low-Wage Industry	13.1	14.5
Medium-Wage Industry	14.8	13.9
High-Wage Industry	29.9	25.9

NOTES: The "Aggregate" figures show average annual percentage changes in federal revenues from the personal income tax that are predicted under the specified policies. "Low-Wage Industry" estimates show how the tax bill of the average worker in low-wage industries would change, and similarly for the "Medium-Wage Industry" and "High-Wage Industry" estimates.

NOTES

[1] Vroman and Anderson (1984) make this point explicitly.

[2] The extra income effect could also be conceptualized as an "endowment" income effect, as Varian (1987) has called it. Oddly, the discussion in Varian's intermediate text appears to be the only full discussion of the endowment income effect in the literature. I am grateful to Carl Davidson for discussion of this point.

[3] Note that whether the *share* of wages increases as the *quantity* of wages increases depends on the relative decrease in the tax-price of wages.

[4] It has usually gone unmentioned that lump-sum taxes are at best difficult to implement, and that efficient government provision of health care services (as of any good or service) entails myriad organizational problems.

[5] The decompositions are shown for each year of the 1969–1982 period. The "Predicted" figures in column (b) are real expenditures (or quantities) predicted by our model for each year under tax reform (with health insurance untaxed), and the "Simulated: Relative Prices, $P*$, and m Changed" figures in column (e) are real expenditures (or quantities) simulated under tax reform with health insurance taxed.

[6] Adamache and Sloan's (1985) estimate is far larger, and Phelps (1984–85) offered no directly comparable estimate.

[7] The decompositions are shown for each year of the 1969–1982 period. The "Predicted" figures in column (b) are real expenditures (or quantities) predicted by our model for each year under tax reform (with fringe benefits untaxed), and the "Simulated: Relative Prices, $P*$, and m Changed" figures in column (e) are real expenditures (or quantities) simulated under tax reform with fringe benefits taxed.

5

Summary and Conclusions

Our goal in this monograph has been to explore the implications for fringe benefits and tax revenues of three major changes in tax policy. The first major change we consider is the 1986 tax reform, which significantly lowered the marginal tax rates on wage income facing most households in the United States. The second is a policy of treating employer contributions to health insurance as taxable income. We consider separately the consequences of taxing all employer contributions, and of taxing only health insurance contributions over $1,125 annually. The final policy we consider is treating all employer contributions to both pensions and health insurance as taxable income. The latter two changes would contrast sharply with the current tax-favored status that employer contributions to pensions and health insurance have enjoyed in the U.S.

The Model

The approach we have taken is to estimate a consumer theoretic model of fringe benefits that takes account of the possibilities for substitution among wages, pension benefits, and health insurance benefits. The model, which is set out in detail in chapter 2, assumes that the employer offers a menu of compensation packages to workers, who select the package that maximizes their well-being. The menu offered by employers implies certain tradeoffs between components of compensation that the employer is willing to make, and these tradeoffs depend in turn on the employer's cost of providing each benefit. The package that workers choose from the menu depends on their preferences (which depend in part on characteristics such as age and marital status), on their level of total compensation, and on the prices of the components of compensation. The prices facing workers depend both on the employer's costs of providing each type of benefit and on the differential tax treatment of each benefit.

More formally, we follow Deaton and Muellbauer (1980a) and specify a flexible expenditure function that yields the following system of demand equations for wages, pensions, and health insurance benefits:

$$s_w = a_w + b_{wr} ln(p_r/p_w) + b_{wh} ln(p_h/p_w) + \qquad (2.33)$$
$$b_w ln(m/P^*) + d_{w1} x_1 + \ldots + d_{wK} x_K + u_w$$

$$s_r = a_r + b_{rr} ln(p_r/p_w) + b_{rh} ln(p_h/p_w) + \qquad (2.34)$$
$$b_r ln(m/P^*) + d_{r1} x_1 + \ldots + d_{rK} x_K + u_r$$

$$s_h = a_h + b_{rh} ln(p_r/p_w) + b_{hh} ln(p_h/p_w) + \qquad (2.35)$$
$$b_h ln(m/P^*) + d_{h1} x_1 + \ldots + d_{hK} x_K + u_h.$$

This is a standard set of demand equations, in the sense that the demand for each component of compensation is modeled as a function of the prices of those benefits, income, and other characteristics such as age and gender. In these equations, s_w, s_r, and s_h are the shares (or proportions) of total compensation received in the form of wages, pension contributions, and health insurance benefits; (p_r/p_w) and (p_h/p_w) are the prices of pensions and health insurance, relative to wages, that face workers; m is total compensation in dollars; P^* is a price index approximated by $ln\ P^* = s_w ln\ p_w + s_r ln\ p_r + s_h ln\ p_h$; x_1 through x_K are control variables other than prices and income, such as demographic characteristics, that might affect the demand for fringe benefits; and u_w, u_r, and u_h, are random disturbance terms that are assumed to be normally distributed with zero mean.

The a_i, b_{ij}, and b_i are parameters that, once estimated, can be converted into the price, income, and substitution elasticities that are needed to determine the effect of changing tax policy on the provision of the different forms of compensation (see chapter 2). The d_{ik} show the influence of the demographic and other characteristics on each compensation share, all else equal.

Two further aspects of this model deserve mention. First, the relative prices in the demand system take account of both the employer's cost of providing each component of compensation, and the tax treatment of each component. Specifically, the relative prices are defined by:

$$p_w/p_r = (c_w/c_r)/(1-t), \qquad (2.5)$$

and

$$p_w/p_h = (c_w/c_h)/(1-t), \qquad (2.36)$$

where c_w, c_r, and c_h are the employer's cost of providing a unit of pension benefits, a unit of wage benefits, and a unit of health insurance benefits; and t is the marginal tax on income faced by the worker. Measurement of these relative prices is an important part of the work (see the appendix to chapter 3).

Second, earlier work on fringe benefits has examined only the choice between wages and fringe benefits taken as a whole. The demand system set out above specifies separate equations for pensions and health insurance, and hence allows examination of tradeoffs within the fringe benefit package.

Summary of Basic Estimates

In chapter 3, we report the results of estimating the model specified above using two entirely different data sets. The first is a pooled time-series of cross sections for 1969–1982 created from the unpublished two-digit industry data underlying the National Income and Product Accounts "other labor income" series (U.S. Department of Commerce, Bureau of Economic Analysis, 1986), and supplementary data bases. The second is a data base created from the 1977 Survey of Employer Expenditures for Employee Compensation (EEEC), the Current Population Survey, and supplementary data bases. We use two separate data bases in exploring tradeoffs among wages, pensions, and health insurance, because each data base has different advantages and disadvantages, and we are able to check the results of the two analyses against each other.

Our two empirical investigations agree in most important respects. In particular, they agree on the effects of income and prices (or taxes) on the mix of compensation, as follows:

(a) The demand for wage benefits is income inelastic, whereas the demand for pensions and health insurance is income elastic. Hence, a doubling of total compensation would result in less than a doubling of wage benefits, whereas the same doubling of income would more than double pension and health insurance benefits.

(b) Both pensions and health insurance are good substitutes for wage benefits and pensions are probably a better substitute for wages than are health insurance benefits. These inferences are based on point estimates of the elasticities of substitution between wages and pensions and between wages and health insurance. Formal statistical tests lend only weak support to the notion that the elasticity of substitution between wages and pensions exceeds that between wages and health insurance.

(c) Evidence on whether pensions and health insurance are substitutes or complements is relatively weak. Findings from both data sets suggest that pensions and health insurance may be complements, but in no case do statistical tests offer a strong rejection of the hypothesis that the elasticity of substitution between pensions and health insurance is zero.

It is important that the two separate investigations offer similar results about the effects of income and prices on the mix of total compensation, because these are the influences on fringe benefits that have changed most over the last 20 years. Also, it is through income and price effects that changes in tax policy make their mark on the mix of total compensation.

The two empirical analyses are in somewhat less agreement on the effects of other variables on the mix of compensation. Nevertheless, several findings in common emerge, and these can be summarized as follows.

(a) Older workers tend to receive a greater share of compensation as pensions, other things equal. But our empirical work is inconclusive about whether older workers receive more or less health insurance, other things equal.

(b) Blue-collar workers tend to receive a greater share of compensation as pensions, other things equal. But again, our empirical work is inconclusive about whether blue-collar workers receive more or less health insurance.

(c) Greater firm-specific skill increases the pension share of total compensation, and has a greater positive effect on pensions than on health insurance. This finding strongly supports the so-called agency hypothesis—that employers use deferred compensation such as pensions to create a bond between the firm and workers who have skills that can be acquired only through tenure with the firm.

(d) When we define the unit of observation as the household (as we are able to do in one of our investigations), we find that women receive a smaller share of their compensation as both pensions and health insurance, other things equal. This finding suggests the importance of including fringe benefits in future analyses of earnings differences between men and women. It also may imply that women tend to rely on the fringe benefits of other household members.

(e) In contrast to previous findings, our findings on the relationship between establishment size and the mix of compensation suggest that firm size plays a limited role in the provision of fringe benefits. This surprising finding suggests that the positive relationship between firm size and fringe benefit provision found in previous studies may be the result of an inability to control fully for income, tax-price, and other influences, and also suggests the importance of further research on the relationship between firm size and benefit provision.

Policy Simulations

In chapter 4, we report simulations of the effects on compensation of three alternative changes in tax policy: (a) the 1986 tax reform; (b) treating employer contributions to health insurance as taxable income (both a policy of taxing all health insurance contributions, and a policy of taxing only contributions over $1,125 annually); and (c) treating all employer contributions to both pensions and health insurance as taxable income. These simulations are based on the modeling and estimation reported in chapters 3 and 4.

Effects of Policy Changes on Compensation

Tables 5.1 and 5.2 summarize the effects of the policy changes on compensation. Table 5.1 shows how each of the four simulated policy changes would have altered real expenditures on each form of compensation and compensation shares *if the policies had been in effect during 1969 through 1982*. All effects are shown in percentage terms, averaged over the 1969–1982 period. Panel A shows the total effects of the policy changes—that is, the sum of the substitution, ordinary income, and extra income effects. Panel B isolates the substitution effects of each policy change—that is, the effect of each policy if only the change in tax-price implied by each were to occur (and if real total compensation and all other independent variables were held constant).

In contrast, table 5.2 shows our estimates of how each policy change would affect real expenditures on compensation and compensation shares *if enacted under the existing tax system*. (Note that the 1986 tax reform is not shown in table 5.2 because comparison of each policy change is with respect to the tax system implied by the 1986 reform.) Again, all changes are shown in percentage terms, and Panel A shows the total effects of each policy change, whereas Panel B shows the substitution effects.

1. *Effects of the 1986 Tax Reform.* Our simulations suggest the following effects of the 1986 tax reform (see table 5.1). First, and most important, the tax reform can be expected to lead to significant *increases* in real expenditures and the share of compensation taken as health insurance. This increase in health insurance occurs in spite of the reduced incentive to receive compensation as health insurance that results from lower marginal tax rates on wages (that is, in spite of a negative substitution effect). *The increase in health insurance is attributable to the large income effects of the tax reform.*

**Table 5.1 Summary of Effects of Policy Changes on Fringe Benefit Provision:
Average Percentage Changes Under Tax Systems Existing 1969–1982**

Panel A: Total Effects

Policy	Wages	Pensions	Health Insurance
Effects of 1986 Tax Reform on:			
Real Expenditures	9.4	0.9	10.4
Compensation Shares	−0.3	−1.4	7.7
Effects of Taxing Health Insurance Contributions on:			
Real Expenditures	−1.8	−5.8	−22.3
Compensation Shares	0.2	−4.7	2.2
Effects of Low Tax Cap on Health Insurance on:			
Real Expenditures	−0.4	−2.6	−13.9
Compensation Shares	0.1	−1.8	0.7
Effects of Taxing All Benefits on:			
Real Expenditures	−0.8	−64.1	−27.9
Compensation Shares	3.0	−53.9	−2.4

Panel B: Substitution Effects

Policy	Wages	Pensions	Health Insurance
Effects of 1986 Tax Reform on:			
Real Expenditures	1.6	−18.5	−6.1
Compensation Shares	0.7	−13.1	0.7
Effects of Taxing Health Insurance Contributions on:			
Real Expenditures	1.0	2.8	−16.9
Compensation Shares	−0.2	−0.6	4.6
Effects of Low Tax Cap on Health Insurance on:			
Real Expenditures	0.7	1.6	−11.3
Compensation Shares	−0.1	−0.4	1.8
Effects of Taxing All Benefits on:			
Real Expenditures	4.3	−53.9	−18.2
Compensation Shares	2.4	−46.1	2.4

SOURCES: Tables 4.1, 4.5, 4.10, and 4.12.

NOTES: The figures show how replacing the tax systems in effect during 1969 through 1982 with the specified tax-policy changes would have changed real expenditures on compensation and shares of compensation. Changes are shown in annual percentage terms, averaged over the 14 years. The total effects show the sum of the substitution, ordinary income, and extra income effects. The substitution effects isolate the impact of the changing tax-price of wages, pensions, and health insurance implied by each policy change.

Table 5.2 Summary of Effects of Policy Changes on Fringe Benefit Provision: Average Percentage Changes under 1986 Tax Reform

Panel A: Total Effects

Policy	Wages	Pensions	Health Insurance
Effects of Taxing Health Insurance Contributions on:			
Real Expenditures	−0.7	−4.3	−14.7
Compensation Shares	0.1	−3.7	1.8
Effects of Low Tax Cap on Health Insurance on:			
Real Expenditures	−0.1	−1.7	−8.7
Compensation Shares	0.0	−1.5	0.4
Effects of Taxing All Benefits on:			
Real Expenditures	−0.4	−48.8	−20.1
Compensation Shares	2.2	−39.3	−1.6

Panel B: Substitution Effects

Policy	Wages	Pensions	Health Insurance
Effects of Taxing Health Insurance Contributions on:			
Real Expenditures	0.7	0.1	−11.9
Compensation Shares	−0.1	−1.5	3.1
Effects of Low Tax Cap on Health Insurance on:			
Real Expenditures	0.4	0.2	−7.4
Compensation Shares	−0.0	−0.6	1.0
Effects of Taxing All Benefits on:			
Real Expenditures	3.4	−38.7	−12.1
Compensation Shares	1.7	−33.8	1.4

SOURCES: Tables 4.6, 4.11, and 4.13.

NOTES: The figures show how the specified tax-policy changes under the 1986 tax reform would change real expenditures on compensation and shares of compensation. The total effects show the sum of the substitution, ordinary income, and extra income effects. The substitution effects isolate the impact of the changing tax-price of wages, pensions, and health insurance implied by each policy change.

Second, the 1986 tax reform will shift the mix of compensation away from pensions and toward health insurance.

Our basic predictions—that the reform will (a) increase real expenditures on health insurance and the share of compensation taken as health insurance, and (b) shift the mix of compensation away from pensions and toward health insurance—can be explained by noting three points. First, as already noted, the tax reform has large income effects that increase the demand for health insurance. Second, the demand for health insurance contributions is inelastic, or unresponsive to changes in tax-prices. Hence, raising the tax-price of health insurance will increase the share of compensation received as health insurance. Third, workers are very willing to substitute back and forth between pensions and wages. That is, the demand for pensions is highly elastic, or responsive to changes in tax-prices. It follows that raising the tax-price of pensions will reduce real expenditures on pension compensation.

The results of simulating the 1986 tax reform are troubling because they suggest that it will be difficult to bring down health insurance expenditures or the health insurance share of compensation. Indeed, because the 1986 tax reform entailed such large income effects, it has likely been an underlying cause of recent increases in the demand for health insurance, even though it has reduced the tax incentives to demand health insurance.

2. *Effects of Taxing Health Insurance Contributions.* Our simulations suggest that treating all health insurance contributions as taxable income would have a strong effect on the provision of health insurance by employers. Taxing health insurance during the 1969–1982 period would have reduced real expenditures on employer-provided health insurance by over 22 percent (table 5.1), and taxing health insurance under the current system could be expected to reduce real expenditures on employer-provided health insurance by nearly 15 percent (table 5.2).

Similarly, taxing health insurance contributions in excess of $1,125 annually (in 1982 dollars) would substantially reduce real expenditures on employer-provided health insurance. Such a policy during the 1969–

1982 period would have reduced real expenditures on health insurance by nearly 14 percent (table 5.1), and doing so under the current tax system would reduce real expenditures on health insurance by nearly 9 percent (table 5.2).

An apparent side effect of taxing health insurance contributions would be a reduction in real expenditures on wages and pensions provided by employers. These decreases result because taxing health insurance would reduce real incomes, which would lead in turn to reductions in both wages and pensions. Although neither reduction would be enormous, the decrease in pension provision should be considered in any public discussion of the merits of taxing health insurance, and ways of offsetting the decrease might be considered if it were viewed as undesirable.

3. *Effects of Taxing All Fringe Benefit Contributions.* Our simulations imply that treating all employer contributions to pensions and health insurance as taxable income would dramatically reduce the provision of both pensions and health insurance. Taxing all fringe benefits would have cut pension provision by 64 percent during the 1969–1982 period, and would cut pensions nearly in half under the current tax system. Health insurance would have been reduced by nearly 14 percent during the 1969–1982 period, and would fall by 20 percent under the current system. These results suggest that reforming the tax system to include employer contributions to both pensions and health insurance as taxable income would be politically difficult.

Another consequence of taxing all fringe benefits would be a major shift in the mix of compensation away from pensions and health insurance and toward wages. The share of compensation received as pensions would be most affected—our simulations suggest a decrease in the pension share of nearly 40 percent.

Pensions are devastated by taxing all fringe benefits, but health insurance is cut by only 20 percent, for a simple reason: Pensions and wages are better substitutes than are health insurance and wages. It follows that when pensions are taxed, workers are readily willing to substitute wages for pensions, but less willing to substitute wages for health insurance.

Effects of Policy Changes on Revenues

Appendix table A4.1 shows how each tax policy change considered would alter revenues collected under the federal personal income tax. All changes are in percentage terms, and the table shows both aggregate revenue effects and the effects on the tax bill of the average worker in low-wage, medium-wage, and high-wage industries. (We consider these industry disaggregations under "Distributional Effects" below.)

The 1986 tax reform is predicted to decrease revenues from the federal personal income tax by over 21 percent (top panel of table A4.1). Interestingly, this revenue loss could be nearly recouped by taxing all fringe benefits—the simulations suggest that taxing all fringe benefits under the current system would increase revenues by 17.6 percent (bottom right panel of table A4.1).

The simulated revenue effects of taxing only employer contributions to health insurance are less dramatic, but appear substantial nevertheless. Taxing all health insurance contributions under the current system would increase income tax revenues by over 8 percent annually. Taxing health contributions over $1,125 would increase income tax revenues by 1.5 percent.

Distributional Effects of the Policy Changes

The distributional effects of the tax policy changes can be seen in two ways. Table A4.1 shows the effect of each policy change on the tax bill of the average worker in low-wage, medium-wage, and high-wage industries. Table 5.3 disaggregates the total effects of each policy change into effects on workers in low-wage, medium-wage, and high-wage industries.

The simulations suggest that the effects of the 1986 tax reform are roughly proportional across industries. Both the revenue effects and the

Table 5.3 Effects of Policy Changes on Real Expenditures on Components of Compensation, by Industry Group

Panel A: Average Percentage Changes Under Tax Systems Existing 1969–1982

Policy/Industry	Wages	Pensions	Health Insurance
1986 Tax Reform:			
Aggregate	9.4	0.9	10.4
Low-Wage Industries	5.0	1.9	8.2
Medium-Wage Industries	8.9	0.5	11.3
High-Wage Industries	13.5	0.7	10.4
Taxing Health Insurance Contributions:			
Aggregate	−1.8	−5.8	−22.3
Low-Wage Industries	−0.7	−1.9	−20.0
Medium-Wage Industries	−1.5	−6.0	−19.9
High-Wage Industries	−2.9	−5.6	−26.2
Low Tax Cap on Health Insurance:			
Aggregate	−0.4	−2.6	−13.9
Low-Wage Industries	−0.0	−0.6	−2.5
Medium-Wage Industries	−0.0	−1.5	−7.4
High-Wage Industries	−1.1	−3.7	−22.3
Taxing All Benefits:			
Aggregate	−0.8	−64.1	−27.9
Low-Wage Industries	0.8	−81.1	−19.8
Medium-Wage Industries	−0.2	−70.2	−24.9
High-Wage Industries	−3.0	−57.2	−32.7

Panel B: Percentage Changes Under 1986 Tax Reform

Policy/Industry	Wages	Pensions	Health Insurance
Taxing Health Insurance Contributions:			
Aggregate	−0.7	−4.3	−17.3
Low-Wage Industries	−0.4	−5.9	−12.8
Medium-Wage Industries	−0.5	−4.7	−13.9
High-Wage Industries	−1.1	−3.7	−15.9
Low Tax Cap on Health Insurance:			
Aggregate	−0.1	−1.7	−8.7
Low-Wage Industries	−0.0	−0.5	−1.7
Medium-Wage Industries	−0.0	−0.9	−5.1
High-Wage Industries	−0.3	−2.5	−13.5
Taxing All Benefits:			
Aggregate	−0.4	−48.8	−20.1
Low-Wage Industries	−0.9	−68.4	−15.9
Medium-Wage Industries	−0.7	−52.3	−16.7
High-Wage Industries	−2.8	−42.9	−23.9

SOURCES: Tables 4.1, 4.5, 4.6, 4.10, 4.11, 4.12, and 4.13.

NOTES: The figures show how the specified tax policy changes would alter real expenditures on compensation. Panel A shows changes under the tax systems in effect during 1969–1982. Panel B shows changes under the current tax system. All changes are total effects (sum of substitution, ordinary income, and extra income effects) in annual percentage terms.

effects of the reform on compensation appear to be similar across industries.

Similarly, the distributional effects of taxing all health insurance contributions are not dramatic. Workers in low-wage industries would experience somewhat smaller decreases in wages and health insurance than workers in high-wage industries. Also, workers in high-wage industries would experience somewhat larger increases in their income tax bills. But the differences among the three groups of workers are not great.

In contrast, the distributional effects of taxing health insurance contributions over $1,125 are significant. Under the low tax cap, workers in high-wage industries would experience a 13.5 percent decrease in health insurance, whereas workers in low- and medium-wage industries would experience a decrease of only 2 to 5 percent. Also, the income taxes of workers in high-wage industries would rise by over 4 percent, whereas the income taxes of other workers would rise by less than 1 percent. We conclude that a low tax cap on health insurance has distributional effects that would increase income equality.

Similarly, the simulations suggest that taxing all health insurance contributions would tend to increase income equality. Workers in low-wage industries would experience income tax increases of 14 to 15 percent, whereas workers in high-wage industries would experience tax increases of nearly 26 percent.

Implications for Public Policy

A multitude of public policy issues currently surround the tax treatment of employee benefits. In particular, the tax-favored status of employer contributions to pensions and health insurance has been blamed for numerous ills: a shrinking tax base that has exacerbated the federal budget deficit; an inefficient and bloated health care sector, overinsurance by many recipients of employer-provided health insurance, and rising health care costs; and a tax system that is made more regressive because those who receive tax-favored fringe benefits tend to be in higher-income households than those who do not.

In addition to being held responsible for these perceived ills, the tax-favored status of fringe benefits is implicitly blamed for failing to solve completely the problems one would expect it to address. Why do some workers still lack health insurance coverage? Why do many lack private pensions? Why, if tax-favored treatment of pension contributions is responsible for the growth of private pensions, is the rate of private saving in the United States nevertheless so low by international standards?

Some Options

Policies suggested to deal with these perceived problems have often addressed one problem without handling another. Two such proposals are (1) taxing all employer contributions to pensions and health insurance, and (2) requiring employers to provide some minimum level of health insurance to all employees—mandated health benefits. We discuss each in turn.

1. *Taxing All Fringe Benefit Contributions.* We suggest that the taxation of all employee benefits is too sweeping a policy change to implement in the foreseeable future. Our estimates suggest that taxing all employer contributions would cut in half employer contributions to private pension plans. Perhaps the simplest implication of this finding is that a policy of taxing all fringe benefits would be politically difficult to implement.

Even if it were not a politically difficult option, our findings suggest that taxing all benefits would dramatically reduce retirement saving through the private pension system, and it is not at all clear that this would be desirable. First, the U.S. economy has a low rate of private saving by international standards, and a policy that would further reduce private saving would be counter to the goal of long-run economic growth (Seidman 1990). Second, taxing all benefits would, by cutting in half the size of private pension contributions, place on the public retirement system an increased long-run burden. If policymakers wish to tax pension contributions, they must in turn be willing either to increase the size of the social security system, or to see the income replacement rates of retirees fall substantially. Neither of these alternatives seems desirable or easy to defend.

In short, because its effects on the private pension system appear to be so dramatic, the policy of taxing all fringe benefits seems both politically infeasible and economically unwise.

2. *Mandated Benefits*. The idea of mandating health benefits has recently caught the attention of the public and many policymakers. A full treatment of mandated health benefits is beyond the scope of this discussion, but three points should be made. First, discussions of mandated benefits often seem to imply that mandating would do away with the problem of uninsured *individuals*, when of course mandating would only do away with the problem of uninsured *workers*. It follows that mandated health insurance is an incomplete policy that would need to be supplemented by a large and expensive public program of health care provision to individuals who would remain uninsured. Only rarely have advocates of mandated health insurance clearly specified the nature of the problem posed by the uninsured, or clearly delineated who would and who would not benefit from mandated benefits (but see Goddeeris 1991). The degree to which mandating would be an efficient way of solving the social problem posed by uninsured individuals is largely an unanswered question.

Second, the effects of mandated benefits on labor markets, especially low-wage labor markets, have yet to be examined in any systematic way. It seems likely that mandated benefits could have the same adverse effects on employment of low-wage workers as a large increase in the minimum wage, but the needed research on this question does not exist.

Third, mandating health care benefits could contribute to further increases in health care costs, and further inefficient use of the health care system. The reason is that, to the extent mandating is successful in extending health insurance to currently uninsured workers and households, it would increase use of the health care system. In part, such an increase would be desirable, but (depending on the package of benefits mandated) it is also possible that further overuse of health services would result.

We conclude that the case for mandating health insurance benefits is far from clear-cut at this time. Too little research, either theoretical or empirical, has been conducted to offer a well-reasoned judgement. What is clear is that mandating benefits, like the favorable tax treatment of health insurance contributions, may create its own set of problems without providing a complete solution to the problems it is intended to address.

A Proposal for Marginal Change

We believe that a relatively low tax cap on health insurance contributions would be a sensible and efficiency-improving policy. A policy of taxing employer contributions to health insurance in excess of a relatively low amount ($1,125 annually, for example, as simulated in chapter 4) has at least five points in its favor.

First, it partially addresses the problems of rising health care costs, overuse of the health care system, and an inefficiently large health care sector. It does so by reducing the incentive for employers to provide compensation in the form of health insurance beyond a given level. As a result, the health insurance provided by employers would be more likely to be true insurance against large and unexpected health expenses, rather than simply a tax subsidy to consumption of health care services that are regular and predictable.

Second, a low tax cap on health insurance addresses the concern that the tax base will continue to be eroded as health care costs rise, and as employer contributions to health insurance increase. Many predictions, including ours, suggest that employer contributions to health insurance will continue to rise in real terms. By limiting the extent to which employer contributions to health insurance are excluded from the tax base, erosion of the tax base would be halted.

Third, a low tax cap on health insurance would *not* limit or reduce access to *basic* health care by any currently insured or potentially insurable worker. It would likely reduce the degree to which workers who are currently overinsured consume health care services. That is, it would tend to reduce the provision by employers of extremely generous insurance that covers regular and predictable health care (Phelps 1984–85). But again, the low tax cap would be unlikely to reduce workers' coverage by employer-provided major medical insurance.

Fourth, in reducing the provision of health insurance for regular and predictable health care, the low tax cap would imply an improvement in the equity of the tax system. Our simulations suggest strongly that a low tax cap on health insurance contributions would have a favorable distributional impact. Because workers who have the highest total compensation tend to be covered by the most generous employer-provided health insurance, taxing health contributions over a specified maximum would be a progressive tax measure.

Fifth, a low tax cap on health insurance contributions would not foreclose the option of mandating health insurance benefits, should policymakers choose to pursue mandating. If all health insurance contributions were taxed, it would be extremely awkward to mandate health insurance coverage because the two policies would tend to work at cross purposes. Taxing benefits above the mandated level would not pose this problem, however. Essentially, a policy of mandating *with* taxation of benefits over a specified level could be viewed as a statement of what level of health insurance benefits is in the public interest. But again, the case for mandating health insurance is not clear-cut at present.

In short, a low tax cap on health insurance contributions would tend to alleviate each of the perceived problems outlined above without exacerbating other problems or shutting out other policy options. Accordingly, we believe the low tax cap to be a sensible and economically sound policy, and would urge its adoption.

References

Adamache, Killard W. and Frank A. Sloan. "Fringe Benefits: To Tax or Not to Tax?" *National Tax Journal* 38 (March 1985): 47–64.

Allen, Steven G. and Robert L. Clark. "Pensions and Firm Performance." In *Human Resources and the Performance of the Firm*, edited by Morris M. Kleiner, Richard N. Block, Myron Roomkin, and Sidney W. Salsburg. Madison, WI: Industrial Relations Research Association, 1987. Pp. 195–242.

Alpert, William T. "Unions and Private Wage Supplements." *Journal of Labor Research* 3 (Spring 1982): 179–199.

Alpert, William T. "Manufacturing Workers' Private Wage Supplements: A Simultaneous Equations Approach." *Applied Economics* 15 (June 1983): 363–378.

Alpert, William T. "An Analysis of Fringe Benefits Using Time Series Data." *Applied Economics* 19 (January 1987): 1–16.

Anderson, Gordon and Richard Blundell. "Testing Restrictions in a Flexible Dynamic Demand System." *Review of Economic Studies* 50 (July 1983): 397–410.

Anderson, Gordon and Richard Blundell. "Consumer Non-Durables in the U.K.: A Dynamic Demand System." *Economic Journal* 94 (Supplement 1984): 35–44.

Anderson, Richard G. and Jerry G. Thursby. "Confidence Intervals for Elasticity Estimators in Translog Models." *Review of Economics and Statistics* 68 (November 1986): 647–656.

Antos, Joseph R. "Wages and Compensation of White-Collar Workers." BLS Working Paper 123, Bureau of Labor Statistics, U.S. Department of Labor, Washington, D.C., 1981.

Antos, Joseph R. "Analysis of Labor Cost: Data Concepts and Sources." In *The Measurement of Labor Cost*, edited by Jack E. Triplett. Chicago: University of Chicago Press and NBER, 1983. Pp. 153–172.

Atrostic, B.K. "Comment on Leibowitz." In *The Measurement of Labor Cost*, edited by Jack E. Triplett. Chicago: University of Chicago Press and NBER, 1983. Pp. 389–394.

167

Atrostic, B. K. and Len Burman. "Report to the Congress on Certain Employee Benefits Not Subject to Federal Income Tax." Office of Tax Analysis, U.S. Department of the Treasury, June 1988.

Bell, David N. F. and Robert A. Hart. "Effort, Worker Quality, Wage Rates, and Firm-Specific Training." Discussion Paper, Department of Economics, University of Stirling, 1990.

Birnbaum, Jeffrey H. "Revenue Hunt: With Tax-Rise Talk Reviving, Legislators Line Up Candidates." *Wall Street Journal*, January 6, 1989, p. 1.

Burkhauser, Richard V. and John A. Turner. "Is the Social Security Payroll Tax a Tax?" *Public Finance Quarterly* 13 (July 1985): 253–267.

Burtless, Gary and Jerry A. Hausman. "The Effect of Taxation on Labor Supply: Evaluating the Gary Negative Income Tax Experiment." *Journal of Political Economy* 86 (December 1978): 1103–1130.

Cantor, J. C. *National Medical Care Expenditure Survey Health Insurance/Employer Survey Data: Person Record Public Use Tape Documentation for Premium Data and Benefit Data*. Rockville, MD: National Center for Health Services Research and Health Care Technology Assessment, 1986.

Chollet, Deborah J. *Employer-Provided Health Benefits*. Washington, D.C.: Employee Benefits Research Institute, 1984.

Christensen, Laurits R. and Marilyn E. Manser. "Cost-of-Living Indexes and Price Indexes for U.S. Meat and Produce, 1947–1971." In *Household Production and Consumption*, edited by Nestor E. Terleckyj. New York: Columbia University Press and NBER, 1976. Pp. 399–446.

Christensen, Laurits R. and Marilyn E. Manser. "Estimating U.S. Consumer Preferences for Meat with a Flexible Utility Function." *Journal of Econometrics* 5 (January 1977): 37–53.

Congressional Budget Office. *Tax Policy for Pensions and Other Retirement Saving*. Washington, D.C.: Congress of the United States, Congressional Budget Office, April 1987.

Deaton, Angus and John Muellbauer. 1980a. "An Almost Ideal Demand System." *American Economic Review* 70 (June 1980): 312–326.

Deaton, Angus and John Muellbauer. 1980b. *Economics and Consumer Behavior*. Cambridge: Cambridge University Press, 1980.

Feldstein, Martin S. "The Welfare Loss of Excess Health Insurance." *Journal of Political Economy* 81 (March/April 1973): 251–280.

Freeman, Richard B. "The Effects of Unionism on Fringe Benefits." *Industrial and Labor Relations Review* 34 (July 1981): 489–509.

Goddeeris, John H. "Universal Health Insurance Through Combining Expanded Private Coverage with Public Programs." In *Improving Access to Health Care: What Can the States Do?* edited by S. E.

Berki, John H. Goddeeris, and Andrew J. Hogan. Kalamazoo, MI: W. E. Upjohn Institute for Employment Research, 1991. Forthcoming.

Goldstein, Gerald S. and Mark V. Pauly. "Group Health Insurance as a Local Public Good." In *The Role of Health Insurance in the Health Services Sector*, edited by Richard N. Rosett. New York: Columbia University Press and NBER, 1976. Pp. 73–110.

Gordon, Roger H. "Social Security and Labor Supply Incentives." *Contemporary Policy Issues* (April 1983): 16–22.

Grant, James H. and Daniel S. Hamermesh. "Labor Market Competition Among Youths, White Women, and Others." *Review of Economics and Statistics* 63 (August 1981): 354–360.

Greenberg, Edward, Walker A. Pollard, and William T. Alpert. "Statistical Properties of Data Stretching." *Journal of Applied Econometrics* 4 (October–December 1989): 383–391.

Griliches, Zvi. "Hedonic Price Indexes for Automobiles: An Econometric Analysis of Quality Change." In *Price Indexes and Quality Change*, edited by Zvi Griliches. Cambridge: Harvard University Press, 1971. Pp. 55–87.

Hall, Robert E. "Wages, Income, and Hours of Work in the U.S. Labor Force." In *Income Maintenance and Labor Supply*, edited by Glen G. Cain and Harold W. Watts. New York: Academic Press, 1973. Pp. 102–162.

Hamermesh, Daniel S. "New Measures of Labor Cost: Implications for Demand Elasticities and Nominal Wage Growth." In *The Measurement of Labor Cost*, edited by Jack E. Triplett. Chicago: University of Chicago Press and NBER, 1983. Pp. 287–305.

Hamermesh, Daniel S. and Stephen A. Woodbury. "Taxes, Fringe Benefits, and Faculty." Working Paper No. 3455, National Bureau of Economic Research, September 1990.

Hart, Robert A. *The Economics of Non-Wage Labour Costs*. London: George Allen and Unwin, 1984.

Hart, Robert A., David N. F. Bell, Rudolf Frees, Seiichi Kawasaki, and Stephen A. Woodbury. *Trends in Non-Wage Labor Costs and Their Effects on Employment*. Luxembourg: Office for Official Publications of the European Communities, 1988.

Hausman, Jerry A. "The Econometrics of Nonlinear Budget Sets." *Econometrica* 53 (November 1985): 1255–1282.

Holmer, Martin. "Tax Policy and the Demand for Health Insurance." *Journal of Health Economics* 3 (December 1984): 203–221.

Johnston, J. *Econometric Methods*, third edition. New York: McGraw-Hill, 1984.

Kang, Suk. *Estimation of an Almost Ideal Demand System from Panel Data.* Ph.D. Dissertation, University of Wisconsin-Madison, 1983.

Kasper, Judith A., Louis F. Rossiter, and Renate Wilson. "A Summary of Expenditures and Sources of Payment for Personal Health Services from the National Medical Expenditure Survey." Data Preview 24, National Center for Health Services Research, Rockville, MD, May 1987.

Kasper, J. A., D. C. Walden, and R. Wilson. *National Medical Care Expenditure Survey Household Data: Person Records Documentation and Codebook.* Rockville, MD: National Center for Health Services Research, 1983.

Kmenta, Jan. *Elements of Econometrics*, second edition. New York: Macmillan, 1986.

Korczyk, Sophie M. *Retirement Security and Tax Policy.* Washington, D.C.: Employee Benefit Research Institute, 1984.

Krinsky, Itzhak and A. Leslie Robb. "On Approximating the Statistical Properties of Elasticities." *Review of Economics and Statistics* 68 (November 1986): 715–719.

Lau, Lawrence J., Wuu-Long Lin, and Pan A. Yotopoulos. "The Linear Logarithmic Expenditure System: An Application to Consumption-Leisure Choice." *Econometrica* 46 (July 1978): 843–868.

Lazear, Edward P. "Agency, Earnings Profiles, Productivity, and Hours Restrictions." *American Economic Review* 71 (September 1981): 606–620.

Leibowitz, Arlene. "Fringe Benefits in Employee Compensation." In *The Measurement of Labor Cost*, edited by Jack E. Triplett, 1983. Pp. 371–389.

Lewbel, Arthur. "A Unified Approach to Incorporating Demographic or Other Effects into Demand Systems." *Review of Economic Studies* 52 (January 1985): 1–18.

Long, James E. and Frank A. Scott. "The Income Tax and Nonwage Compensation." *Review of Economics and Statistics* 64 (May 1982): 211–219.

Megdal, Sharon Bernstein. "The Econometrics of Piecewise-Linear Budget Constraints: A Monte Carlo Study." *Journal of Business and Economic Statistics* 5 (April 1987): 243–248.

Mellow, Wesley. "Employer Size, Unionism, and Wages." In *Research in Labor Economics, Supplement 2: New Approaches to Unions*, edited by Ronald G. Ehrenberg. Greenwich, CT: JAI Press, 1983. Pp. 253–282.

Mitchell, Olivia S. "Employee Benefits in the U.S. Labor Market." In *Proceedings of the Fortieth Annual Meeting*, Industrial Relations Research Association. Madison, WI: IRRA, 1988. Pp. 213–219.

Mitchell, Olivia S. and Emily S. Andrews. "Scale Economies in Private Multi-Employer Pension Systems." *Industrial and Labor Relations Review* 34 (July 1981): 522-530.

Moffitt, Robert. "The Econometrics of Piecewise-Linear Budget Constraints: A Survey and Exposition of the Maximum Likelihood Method." *Journal of Business and Economic Statistics* 4 (July 1986): 317-328.

Moffitt, Robert. "The Econometrics of Kinked Budget Constraints." *Journal of Economic Perspectives* 4 (Spring 1990): 119-139.

Moulton, Brent R. "An Illustration of a Pitfall in Estimating the Effects of Aggregate Variables on Micro Units." *Review of Economics and Statistics* 72 (May 1990): 334-338.

Mumy, Gene E. and William D. Manson. "The Relative Importance of Tax and Agency Incentives to Offer Pensions: A Test Using the Impact of ERISA." *Public Finance Quarterly* 13 (October 1985).

Munnell, Alicia H. "Employee Benefits and the Tax Base." *New England Economic Review* (January 1984): 39-55.

Munnell, Alicia H. "The Economic Effects of the Growth of Employer-Provided Fringe Benefits." In *Distribution and Economics of Employer-Provided Fringe Benefits*, Hearings before the Committee on Ways and Means, U.S. House of Representatives, September 17-18, 1984. Washington, D.C.: USGPO, 1985. Pp. 421-428.

Munnell, Alicia H. "Public versus Private Provision of Retirement Income. *New England Economic Review* (May/June 1988): 51-58.

Munnell, Alicia H. "It's Time to Tax Employee Benefits." In *Proceedings of the Forty-First Annual Meeting*, Industrial Relations Research Association. Madison, WI: IRRA, 1989. Pp. 374-386.

Organization for Economic Cooperation and Development. *The Taxation of Fringe Benefits*. Paris: OECD, 1988.

Parsons, Donald O. "Specific Human Capital: An Application to Quit Rates and Layoff Rates." *Journal of Political Economy* 80 (November/December 1972): 1120-1143.

Pechman, Joseph A. *Federal Tax Policy*, third edition, fifth edition. Washington, D.C.: Brookings Institution, 1977, 1987.

Phelps, Charles E. "Taxing Health Insurance: How Much Is Enough?" *Contemporary Policy Issues* 3 (Winter 1984-85): 47-54.

Phlips, Louis. *Applied Consumption Analysis*, revised and enlarged edition. Amsterdam: North-Holland, 1982.

Pollak, Robert A. and Terence J. Wales. "Demographic Variables in Demand Analysis." *Econometrica* 49 (November 1981): 1533-1551.

Rice, Robert G. 1966a. *An Analysis of Private Wage Supplements*. Ph.D. Dissertation, Columbia University, 1966.

Rice, Robert G. 1966b. "Skill, Earnings, and the Growth of Wage Supplements." *American Economic Review* 56 (May 1966): 583–593.

Seidman, Laurence S. *Saving for America's Economic Future*. Armonk, NY: M. E. Sharpe, 1990.

Shephard, Ronald W. *Theory of Cost and Productions*. Princeton, NJ: Princeton University Press, 1970.

Sloan, Frank A. and Killard W. Adamache. "Taxation and the Growth of Nonwage Compensation." *Public Finance Quarterly* 14 (April 1986): 115–137.

Smeeding, Timothy M. "The Size Distribution of Wage and Nonwage Compensation: Employer Cost versus Employee Value." In *The Measurement of Labor Cost*, edited by Jack E. Triplett. Chicago: University of Chicago Press and NBER, 1983. Pp. 237–277.

Smith, Robert S. and Ronald G. Ehrenberg. "Estimating Wage-Fringe Trade-Offs: Some Data Problems." In *The Measurement of Labor Cost*, edited by Jack E. Triplett. Chicago: University of Chicago Press and NBER, 1983. Pp. 347–369.

Stafford, Frank. "Forestalling the Demise of Empirical Economics: The Role of Microdata in Labor Economics Research." In *Handbook of Labor Economics*, edited by Orley Ashenfelter and Richard Layard. Amsterdam: North-Holland, 1986. Pp. 387–423.

Taylor, Amy K. and Gail R. Wilensky. "The Effect of Tax Policies on Expenditures for Private Health Insurance." In *Market Reforms in Health Care*, edited by Jack A. Meyer. Washington, D.C.: American Enterprise Institute, 1983. Pp. 163–184.

Theil, Henri. *The System-Wide Approach to Microeconomics*. Chicago: University of Chicago Press, 1980.

Toevs, Alden L. "Appropriate Variance Formulas for the Elasticities of Substitution Obtained from the Translog Production Functions." *Economic Letters* 5 (1980): 155–160.

Toevs, Alden L. "Appropriate Variance Formulas for the Elasticities of Substitution Obtained from the Translog Production Functions." *Economic Letters* 10 (1982): 107–113.

Triplett, Jack E. "An Essay on Labor Cost." In *The Measurement of Labor Cost*, edited by Jack E. Triplett. Chicago: University of Chicago Press and NBER, 1983. Pp. 1–60.

Turner, Robert W. "Are Taxes Responsible for the Growth in Fringe Benefits?" *National Tax Journal* 40 (June 1987): 205–220.

Varian, Hal R. *Intermediate Microeconomics*. New York: W. W. Norton, 1987.

Vogel, Ronald J. "The Tax Treatment of Health Insurance Premiums as a Cause of Overinsurance." In *National Health Insurance*, edited by Mark V.

Pauly. Washington, D.C.: American Enterprise Institute, 1980. Pp. 220–249.

Vroman, Susan and Gerard Anderson. "The Effects of Income Taxation on the Demand for Employer-Provided Health Insurance." *Applied Economics* 16 (February 1984): 33–43.

Wales, Terence J. "Estimation of a Labor Supply Curve for Self-Employed Business Proprietors." *International Economic Review* 14 (February 1973): 69–80.

Wales, Terence J. and Alan D. Woodland. "Labour Supply and Progressive Taxes." *Review of Economic Studies* 46 (June 1979): 83–95.

Wilensky, Gail R., Pamela J. Farley, and Amy K. Taylor. "Variations in Health Insurance Coverage: Benefits vs. Premiums." *Milbank Memorial Fund Quarterly/Health and Society* 62 (Winter 1984): 53–81.

Woodbury, Stephen A. "Substitution Between Wage and Nonwage Benefits." *American Economic Review* 73 (March 1983): 166–182.

Woodbury, Stephen A. "Taxation and Employer-Provision of Fringe Benefits." Paper presented at the Midwest Economics Association Annual Meeting, Cincinnati, Ohio, March 28–30, 1985.

Woodbury, Stephen A. and Douglas R. Bettinger. "The Decline of Fringe Benefit Coverage in the 1980s." In *Structural Changes in U.S. Labor Markets in the 1980s: Causes and Consequences*, edited by Randall W. Eberts and Erica Groshen. Armonk, NY: M. E. Sharpe, 1991. Pp. 101–134.

Woodbury, Stephen A. and Wei-Jang Huang. "The Slowing Growth of Fringe Benefits." Paper presented at the Eastern Economic Association Annual Convention, Boston, Massachusetts, March 10–12, 1988.

U.S. Department of Commerce, Bureau of the Census. *1970 Census of Population: Subject Reports, Industrial Characteristics*. Washington, D.C.: USGPO, 1972. Table 32.

U.S. Department of Commerce, Bureau of the Census. *1980 Census of Population: Detailed Population Characteristics, United States Summary*. Washington, D.C.: USGPO, 1982. Table 289.

U.S. Department of Commerce, Bureau of the Census. *County Business Patterns (Annual): United States*. Washington, D.C.: USGPO, various years.

U.S. Department of Commerce, Bureau of Economic Analysis. *The National Income and Product Accounts of the United States, 1929–82, Statistical Tables*. Washington, D.C.: USGPO, September 1986.

U.S. Department of Commerce, Bureau of Economic Analysis. *Survey of Current Business*, various July issues.

U.S. Department of Labor, Bureau of Labor Statistics. *Employment and Earnings*. Washington, D.C.: USGPO, various March issues. Tables B-2 and B-3.

U.S. Department of the Treasury, Internal Revenue Service. *Statistics of Income 1977, Individual Income Tax Returns*. Washington, D.C.: USGPO, 1979.

INDEX